LITERARY
BUCKINGHAMSHIRE

PAUL WREYFORD

The
History
Press

First published in the United Kingdom in 2008 by
Sutton Publishing, an imprint of The History Press Limited

Reprinted 2017 by
The History Press
The Mill, Brimscombe Port
Stroud, Gloucestershire, GL5 2QG
www.thehistorypress.co.uk

British Library Cataloguing in Publication Data
A catalogue record for this book is available from the British Library.

ISBN 978 0 7509 4959 0

This book is dedicated to Michella

Typesetting and origination by
The History Press Limited.
Printed in Great Britain by TJ International Ltd, Padstow, Cornwall

Contents

Lavendon
Olney
Newton Blossomville
Weston Underwood
Ravenstone
Gayhurst
North Crawley
Newport Pagnell
Stowe
Stony Stratford
Milton Keynes Village
Water Stratford
Woolstone
Buckingham
Whaddon
Fenny Stratford
Gawcott
Great Horwood
Newton Longville
Adstock
Hillesden
Winslow
Claydons
Stewkley
Swanbourne
Twyford
North Marston
Whitchurch
Wing
Grendon Underwood
Quainton
Hardwick
Mentmore
Weedon
Ludgershall
Waddesdon
Hulcott
Wotton Underwood
Ivinghoe
Boarstall
Aylesbury
Drayton Beauchamp
Little Gaddesden
Oakley
Ashridge
Aldbury
Aston Clinton
Tring
Worminghall
Wendover
Berkhamsted
Ickford
Aston Sandford
Ellesborough
Cholesbury
Thame
Great Kimble
Chesham
Princes Risborough
Great Missenden
Hyde Heath
Crowell
Great Hampden
Latimer
Lacey Green
Speen
Holmer Green
Bradenham
Amersham
Chenies
Chorleywood
Hughenden
Chalfont St Giles
Ibstone
West Wycombe
Penn
Coleshill
Turville
High Wycombe
Beaconsfield
Jordans
Chalfont St Peter
Stonor
Gerrards Cross
Bourne End
Hedsor
Hambleden
Marlow
Farnham Common
Denham
Greenlands
Cliveden
Stoke Poges
Medmenham
Cookham Dean
Burnham
Farnham Royal
Henley-on-Thames
Taplow
Iver

Introduction

Think of Buckinghamshire and you will not immediately think of literature. While many counties are synonymous with a famous writer, or go to great lengths to proclaim scribes for their own, 'beechy Bucks' – as poet John Betjeman fondly called it – has remained largely quiet on the subject in recent years.

Some regions have more than one book devoted to their literary associations, but to my knowledge, this is the first to solely celebrate Buckinghamshire's rich literary heritage. And rich it is indeed. The aim of this book is to prove that the county is just as rich, if not richer, than many of its more prominent neighbours.

Betjeman is perhaps one of the first names many will utter if asked for a famous writer connected with Buckinghamshire. Through his popular television series, *Metroland*, he did much to put the county on the map, but he was by no means the only author to seek solace within its boundaries.

John Milton came here to escape the London plague; Enid Blyton fled the capital's increasing development, while D.H. Lawrence and his German wife took refuge during the outbreak of the First World War – unsuccessfully.

Benjamin Disraeli could not bear to leave his Buckinghamshire home, even for a short spell, while G.K. Chesterton discovered the county by accident and stayed for the rest of his life.

In its landscape, there is perhaps not a more 'English' county. To the north is the Vale of Aylesbury and its fertile pasture lands, while the south is dominated by the beechwoods of the Chiltern Hills. Running along the bottom of the county, acting as a natural border, is the River Thames, where Jerome K. Jerome, Percy Bysshe Shelley and Kenneth Grahame enjoyed 'messing about in boats'.

I have organised the book by splitting the county into seven sections, while there is also a section on some of the literary connections 'just over the border'. This is a comprehensive guide to literary Buckinghamshire, but not an exhaustive one. It would be impossible to include every man and woman of letters to have come here.

Many of the properties that were once home to writers are now private residences and, while I have found the majority of their current owners to be only too delighted to discuss the history of their homes, their privacy should also be respected, should you decide to visit the area yourself. Where properties are open to the public, I have made a point of mentioning this fact.

All pictures are from my own collection. It just remains for me to thank all those who have helped with my research in some way, by answering a question or merely pointing me in the right direction.

1

Cowper Country

The River Great Ouse winds its way through the very northern corner of Buckinghamshire. This is Cowper Country, an area enchanted by a shy and retiring poet who immersed himself in nature and his rural surroundings. He was a man who lamented change and would have been horrified by the emergence of the M1 motorway and the new city of Milton Keynes – with its concrete cows – to the south, but even here, amid the outlining villages, there are literary surprises waiting to be unravelled.

OLNEY

William Cowper

There is no doubting the impact that poet and hymn-writer William Cowper had on this corner of North Buckinghamshire, nor the impact the area had on him.

The region inhabited by this shy and melancholy man of letters is today often marketed as 'Cowper Country', with Olney – the town he lived in for some nineteen years – sitting at its heart. The local landscape inspired Cowper to pen many of his famous nature poems, as well as some of the country's best-loved hymns.

Many who come to the area might think little has changed since Cowper's day, but the poet would probably not agree. In *The Task*, a poem written in the second half of the eighteenth century, when England was largely untouched by modern encroachment, Cowper still talked of change and harked back to the glorious past. 'God made the country, and man made the town,' he famously declared. He lamented the wind of change, with the stagecoach partly to blame, the 'stir of Commerce, driving slow, and thundering loud, with his ten thousand wheels'. He added: 'We have bid farewell to all the virtues of those better days, and all their honest pleasures.'

Despite Cowper's fears of change, he still loved this part of the world with all his heart. *The Task*, written at Olney, fondly describes many local scenes, such as the River Great Ouse.

Cowper came to Olney from Huntingdon following the death, in 1767, of close friend Morley Unwin, a retired Evangelical churchman. His widow, Mary Unwin, came with the poet. Though only a few years his senior, she was like a mother to him.

It was the preacher John Newton, a converted ex-slave trader, who was the curate here, and who persuaded the pair to come. Cowper and Newton were an unlikely partnership, like chalk and cheese, but they combined to produce some of the greatest words in British hymnology.

It is generally accepted that Newton, a radical Calvinist, wrote 280 of the *Olney Hymns*, while Cowper, a reserved and timid man, penned sixty-eight, including *God Moves in a Mysterious Way*. Newton encouraged much of Cowper's poetry. Sadly, his influence was not always beneficial. He used Cowper as a sort of lay curate and the endless visits to the sick, prayer meetings and theological studies took their toll. Cowper, already prone to bouts of depression, continued to suffer from mental illness for the rest of his life. Ironically, he sought comfort from the well-meaning Newton, but his passionate and formidable friend might not have been the best person to turn to, his ravings sowing more seeds of doubt and fears of damnation. A path in the garden of Cowper's house, situated in Market Place, led across a small field to Newton's vicarage and the poet is known to have fled there on at least one occasion when tormented by the demons in his mind. Cowper and Newton paid the owner of an orchard that lay

The Cowper & Newton Museum at Olney.

between their two homes a guinea a year for the privilege of crossing the land to reach each other's garden. It is still known as Guinea Field.

Cowper and Mary lived at Olney for about nineteen years before moving the short distance to the village of Weston Underwood to be closer to the Throckmortons of Weston Hall, their closest friends.

The Olney house in which Cowper lived, Orchard Side, is now a museum dedicated to the life of both the poet and Newton. Visitors can still see the summer house in the garden where Cowper wrote some of his greatest works. He came to the 'verse manufactory', as he called it, after breakfast each day. The poet loved his garden and said 'gardening was, of all employments, that in which I succeeded best'.

One of Cowper's other loves at Olney was his three pet hares. He was given them in the hope they would take his mind off his illness. He built them homes to sleep in and visitors had to enter the house via the kitchen, the front door rarely being opened for fear they would escape. Cowper wrote much about his hares in letters to fellow scribes, including Samuel Taylor Coleridge.

Apart from his hymns, Cowper penned *The Diverting History of John Gilpin* at Olney, though it is *The Task* that best reflects his love of the surrounding countryside. The same views Cowper wrote about can still be seen and, despite his own fears, have changed little.

*The summer house
where Cowper wrote.*

Cowper knew many of the surrounding villages well. It was at Clifton Reynes that the poet first met Lady Austen, the widow of a wealthy baronet, who came here to stay with her sister at the parsonage, the latter's husband being the curate at the time and a friend of Cowper. She told Cowper the story of John Gilpin, which the poet later turned into verse, and set him the challenge of writing about his sofa, which led to him penning his greatest poem – *The Task*.

Cowper also spent many hours visiting the Chesters at Chicheley Hall. He also had friends at Gayhurst, Newport Pagnell and, of course, Weston Underwood, the village he later moved to.

William Cowper's house at Olney became something of a literary shrine following his death and many writers came to pay homage to this great man of letters.

Scottish travel writer Hugh Miller was disappointed when he visited in the nineteenth century to see the house, then a school, much changed and looking a little shabby.

Poet John Betjeman was a twentieth-century visitor, Cowper being one of his favourite poets.

John Newton

It is not surprising that John Newton believed God had shown 'amazing grace' to save 'a wretch like me'.

Few spiritual conversions have been as dramatic as that of the curate of Olney. Newton was a loathsome, foul-mouthed slave trader, but, from his selfish and cruel existence, he became one of the great leaders of the Evangelical Revival, penning one of the country's most famous and best-loved hymns – *Amazing Grace*.

It is believed Newton turned to God following a storm at sea. Fearing death, he pleaded for mercy and, when the storm finally subsided and his life was spared, Newton pledged to dedicate it to his creator, eventually giving up his seafaring exploits for the pulpit.

Newton came under the influence of John Wesley and Charles Wesley, but became an Anglican, rather than a Methodist. He became the curate of Olney in 1764 and spent sixteen years here.

Newton's hymns were first sung on weekday evenings, the singing of hymns in church on Sundays still not being totally acceptable. The popular preacher, who packed out his church, did much to promote hymns as a form of worship. Those evening sessions, such was their popularity, soon had to switch to larger premises.

Newton was a brilliant preacher. His sermons attracted people from far and wide, and he became something of a celebrity. He penned a number of theological works, including a book on ecclesiastical history, though it is for his hymns, such as *How Sweet the Name of Jesus Sounds*, that earned him lasting fame.

Newton also played a big part in ending the slave trade he was once at the heart of. He encouraged William Wilberforce, the Evangelical MP, in his fight to abolish slavery, a bill eventually being passed in 1807.

Newton left Olney in 1780 and died in the London parish he served following his departure, but his body was brought back to Buckinghamshire and he now lies at rest in the churchyard at Olney.

The tomb of John Newton.

The vicar of Olney at the time John Newton was the curate was Moses Browne, himself a writer of poems and plays.

A later vicar was Henry Gauntlett, who served from 1815–33, and published a number of sermons. His son, Henry John Gauntlett, became a famous composer and the editor of psalms and hymn tunes.

Though not born in Olney, Gauntlett Junior spent part of his childhood here and became the organist at St Peter & St Paul's Church. He went on to compose hundreds of hymn tunes and was labelled the 'Father of English Church Music'.

Thomas Scott

John Newton persuaded many to join the Evangelical Revival and Thomas Scott – the man who eventually succeeded him at Olney – was one of them.

Scott, who later gained fame for a commentary on the Bible, was a clergyman who needed to be converted. In his autobiography, *Force of Truth*, which appeared in 1779, Scott wrote that he had no spiritual zeal when he was ordained in the Church of England in his mid-20s. It was not unusual for people to look upon the Church as a career rather than a vocation. Scott was one of many indifferent clergymen and admitted that he took up the career because of the intellectual interest the profession afforded. He took the job as a way of earning a comfortable living and to gain time to continue more interesting studies. Scott revealed that he carried out just enough duties to support a decent character.

But Newton, such was his influence, was to change everything. Scott first came across Newton while serving the parishes of Weston Underwood and Stoke Goldington. At first he regarded his Olney predecessor with disgust and challenged the Evangelical to write an essay about the points they differed on. Scott clearly believed he would win the argument, but, instead, gradually became won over and eventually joined the movement he once so despised.

Scott launched himself into his pastoral labours with added rigour and enthusiasm from that day and went on to become one of the great preachers of the age. However, his efforts appear not to have been appreciated – not at Olney, at any rate. He had a hard act to follow in the charismatic Newton and recorded: 'I am very unpopular in this town, and preach in general to small congregations.' He left Olney for London in 1785. His commentary, written in the capital, was a six-volume attempt to interpret every line of Scripture.

Scott eventually returned to Buckinghamshire and spent his final years serving the people of Aston Sandford, near Haddenham.

William Carey

The Baptist Church at Olney played an important part in the life of William Carey, the father of modern missions.

Though mostly associated with several villages over the border in Northamptonshire, Carey was set apart for the ministry here and met others who co-founded the Baptist Missionary Society (BMS), which still exists today. Pastors John Sutcliff, John Ryland and Andrew Fuller, who was to become the secretary of the mission, were themselves writers of theological works.

Carey's most famous literary work, popularly known as *Enquiry*, was written to encourage missions abroad, though he was also responsible for many Bible translations, making use of his expertise in Indian languages. Carey was the first missionary of the BMS, setting off for India in 1793, the year after the organisation was formed.

Michael Drayton

It is not known whether poet Michael Drayton ever visited Olney, or even Buckinghamshire itself.

Readers of his chief work, *Poly-Olbion*, would assume that he did, but it is thought that most of the material gathered for the epic topographical poem came from written sources. There is no evidence to prove that he travelled to the many places mentioned in his poetical survey of England and Wales.

The work, which Drayton spent much of the early seventeenth century working on, aimed to awaken readers to the splendour of their surroundings. The landscape, sights and history of the country are featured, with particular emphasis on rivers, including the River Great Ouse. Drayton remarks on the fast-flowing river running through Olney: 'Ouse having Olney past, as she were waxed mad.'

Other parts of Buckinghamshire are also mentioned in the work, including Aylesbury Vale, 'that walloweth in her wealth'.

WESTON UNDERWOOD

William Cowper

'The limes and the elms of Weston can witness for us both how often we have sighed and said, Oh that our garden door opened into this grove, or into this wilderness!'

Michael Drayton remarked on the River Great Ouse at Olney.

William Cowper and Mary Unwin long dreamed of living at Weston Underwood, and this became a reality in 1786, after some nineteen years at Olney. Cowper said for many years, the two walked the mile or so from their Olney home every day. Their destination was usually Weston Hall, home of the Throckmortons, their close friends. The renowned Roman Catholic family offered them Weston Lodge, now called Cowper's Lodge, so that they would be closer – not that Cowper dreaded the trek, as his works reveal that he liked nothing better than rambling in the countryside.

Cowper described Weston Underwood as 'one of the prettiest villages in England'. The poet drew inspiration from the land, one of his favourite spots being the Alcove, which was erected by the Throckmortons and can be found in a field half a mile up Wood Lane. Here the writer would sit and draw inspiration from the splendid view. It is said that many of his later works were written here, including his translation of Homer's *Iliad*. A plaque in the Alcove contains some lines from *The Task*, the work that was perhaps most inspired by the Buckinghamshire landscape: 'The summit gained, behold the proud alcove that crowns it.'

Sadly, Cowper's mental problems worsened at Weston Underwood and Mary's health also took a turn for the worse. The poet made at least one suicide attempt here.

Friends decided in the best interests of both, that a complete change of scenery would do them good. So, in 1795, they left for a new life in Norfolk. Cowper loved Buckinghamshire and could not bear to leave. He wrote on a panel of his bedroom window shutter, which can now be found in the museum at Olney, the words: 'Farewell, dear scenes, for ever closed to me; Oh, for what sorrows must I now exchange ye!' His words were sadly prophetic. Cowper's health declined further in Norfolk and he died five years later.

Above: *William Cowper's Weston Underwood home.*

Left: *Cowper came to the Alcove to write.*

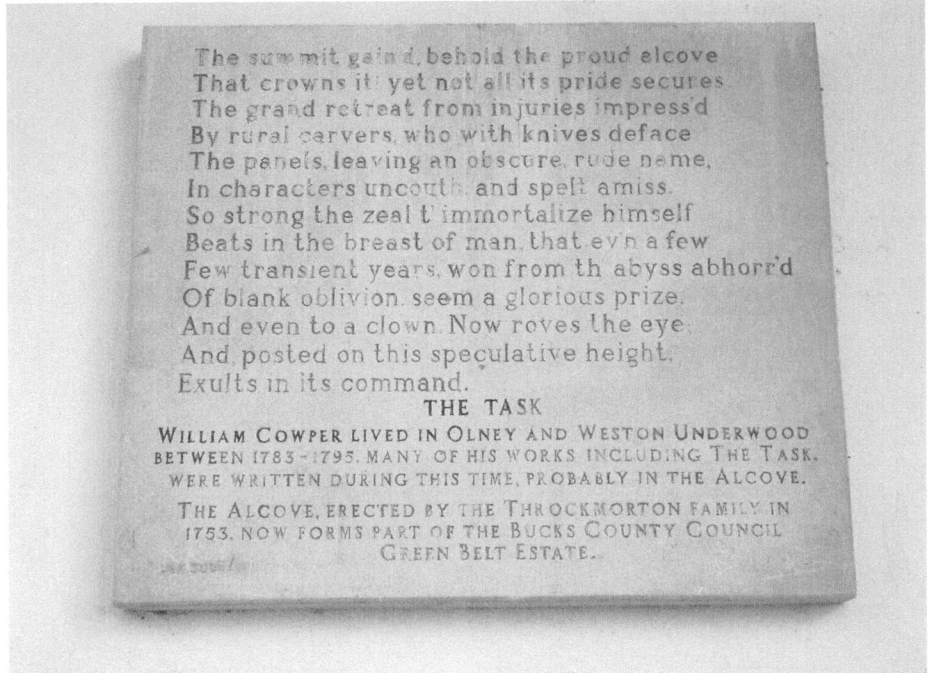

The summit gain'd, behold the proud elcove
That crowns it; yet not all its pride secures
The grand retreat from injuries impress'd
By rural carvers, who with knives deface
The panels, leaving an obscure, rude name,
In characters uncouth, and spelt amiss.
So strong the zeal t'immortalize himself
Beats in the breast of man, that ev'n a few
Few transient years, won from th'abyss abhorr'd
Of blank oblivion, seem a glorious prize.
And even to a clown. Now roves the eye;
And, posted on this speculative height,
Exults in its command.

THE TASK

WILLIAM COWPER LIVED IN OLNEY AND WESTON UNDERWOOD
BETWEEN 1783-1795. MANY OF HIS WORKS INCLUDING THE TASK,
WERE WRITTEN DURING THIS TIME, PROBABLY IN THE ALCOVE.

THE ALCOVE, ERECTED BY THE THROCKMORTON FAMILY IN
1753, NOW FORMS PART OF THE BUCKS COUNTY COUNCIL
GREEN BELT ESTATE.

Words from The Task *can be found in the Alcove.*

Cowper's Lodge remains in the village, but Weston Hall no longer exists. The poet's former home is close to Cowper's Oak, a pub named in honour of a now long-gone ancient tree at nearby Yardley Chase, which inspired one of his poems.

Thomas Scott

Thomas Scott took possession of the joint curacy of Weston Underwood and Stoke Goldington when he first came to the county in the early 1770s. He later also served the people of Ravenstone.

It was at Weston Underwood that he first came under the influence of John Newton, whom he replaced as the curate of Olney in 1781.

RAVENSTONE

Thomas Seaton

The Church of All Saints is the resting place of Thomas Seaton, the man who gave his name to one of the most famous prizes in literature.

The Seatonian Prize for sacred poetry at Cambridge has been awarded since 1750, Christopher Smart having been the first recipient.

Seaton, a religious writer himself, was the vicar of Ravenstone from 1721–41. He turned his pen towards defending the Orthodox Church, as well as producing a number of works on moral and devotional issues.

John Milton

Heneage Finch gave much to the village of Ravenstone, but he is also remembered as the man who tried to hang poet John Milton.

Finch, a Royalist, argued that the writer, a prisoner following the death of Oliver Cromwell, was, in his role as Latin secretary to the great Parliamentarian, a worthy case for the noose. Fortunately for Milton – and literature – the solicitor-general, Finch, who later became Lord Chancellor, never got his way.

Finch's tomb dominates the church at Ravenstone and his legacy is all around. He founded the almshouses close to the church. Samuel Pepys mentioned Finch in his famous diary.

Finch's almshouses at Ravenstone.

LAVENDON

Isaac Newton

Scientist and philosopher Isaac Newton, who gained fame for his theories of gravitation, found the pull of Lavendon Grange too strong to resist. He was a frequent visitor here, the property belonging to relatives. Though not known for his literary output, Newton was still a successful writer, penning many scientific, mathematical, philosophical and religious treatises.

NEWTON BLOSSOMVILLE

William Warburton

Religious controversialist William Warburton was perhaps not the most popular rector to serve the Church of St Nicholas at Newton Blossomville.

Warburton has often been labelled the most quarrelsome literary figure that ever lived. He turned his pen against all who dared criticise him and also launched numerous unprovoked attacks.

Warburton, who served the parish at the beginning of his ecclesiastical career for a short spell from 1726, was mostly concerned with theological issues. He became a bishop in later life and was typical in his reaction against anyone who threatened change within the Church; the Evangelicals and freethinkers being among those he sought issue with. Warburton is best known for *The Divine Legation of Moses*, a work that attempted to show why there was no mention of the afterlife in the Old Testament.

As well as his religious works, Warburton gained fame as the literary executor of Alexander Pope. It is said he persuaded his friend to pen *The New Dunciad*.

NORTH CRAWLEY

John Garbrand

Theologian John Garbrand served as the rector of North Crawley from the mid-1560s until his death in 1589.

Though almost forgotten today, Garbrand was a respected preacher and scholar in his time. He was present at the death of Bishop John Jewel in 1571, the famous defender of the Church of England who bequeathed his papers to Garbrand, who edited some of his works.

James Boswell

The name of Boswell has been associated with North Crawley since the eighteenth century. David Boswell, the younger brother of James, settled at Crawley Grange after returning from abroad. James Boswell is best remembered as the biographer of Samuel Johnson.

GAYHURST

Kenelm Digby

The terrible fate of his father did not dissuade Kenelm Digby from taking up his pen for the Catholic cause.

Digby, who became one of the most remarkable thinkers of the day, was not even 3 years old when Everard Digby was hanged, drawn and quartered for his part in the Gunpowder Plot. Though Digby Junior would not go to such lengths in a bid to see a Catholic monarch restored to the throne, he still devoted much of his life to securing rights for Catholics, and wrote a famous defence of the faith – *A Conference with a Lady About Choice of Religion*. The work, published in the 1630s, argued that the Catholic Church was the only true church. This was a belief shared by his devout father, who is said to have made frequent use of the priest holes and secret passages at the family home in Gayhurst. The impressive manor house became a place for the Catholic conspirators to plot their dastardly deed. Of course, Kenelm, who was born at Gayhurst in 1603, would have been too young to comprehend what his father and friends were concocting.

As an adult, Digby was certainly not as devout as his father and there were some who even questioned whether he was totally sincere in his religious beliefs. The scribe, who came under the tuition of Archbishop William Laud, switched to Anglicanism for a spell, for fear his Catholic upbringing would become a hindrance to his many aspirations. However, he soon reverted back to Catholicism and went on to pen many treatises on the subject.

Gayhurst, home of Kenelm Digby.

As well as being a writer, Digby could list a wide range of occupations during his lifetime, including courtier, naval commander, diplomat, philosopher and scientist. He spent much of his life abroad, often at sea or later in exile. The scribe became a loyal supporter of Charles I and backed the Royalist cause during the Civil War. He later became chancellor to Queen Henrietta Maria when she fled England, something that worked in his favour at the Restoration.

Digby was a versatile writer. As well as his religious works, he also had a great interest in science, alchemy and astrology. He even wrote a cookbook.

Digby was a man torn between the physical and spiritual. He is regarded as the first person to note the importance of oxygen to plants, but believed in the 'powder of sympathy' to heal wounds. The author's treatises on the soul have proved to be more enduring than his scientific ones, but Digby's works, though celebrated in his day, are all now largely forgotten.

Poet and playwright Ben Jonson was one of many writers to immortalise the wife of Kenelm Digby. Venetia Stanley, a well-known intellectual and beauty, turned heads when she was presented to the royal court and had many admirers.

Digby and Venetia were childhood friends, the latter having been brought up by a Catholic family at Salden, a few miles south of Gayhurst, following her mother's death. Both families opposed the attachment and the two eventually wed in secret. After Venetia's premature death in 1633, Jonson (Digby was his literary executor) was one of many poets to dedicate an elegy in her memory. He called Venetia his muse. Dramatist James Shirley is believed to have based *The Wedding* on the couple's situation.

William Cowper was a later visitor to the manor house at Gayhurst. The poet and hymn-writer came with Mary Unwin from their Olney home and was full of praise for the elegant gardens. 'I was delighted at all I found there,' he wrote. Cowper also walked here on other occasions, to exchange seeds with the gardener.

NEWPORT PAGNELL

Samuel Butler

A former worthy of Newport Pagnell is said to have been the chief target in Samuel Butler's most famous attack on Puritanism.

Butler is reputed to have based the title character of the satirical poem *Hudibras* on Samuel Luke, the Presbyterian knight and governor of the town during the Civil War.

The writer served Luke, whose home was at Cople in Bedfordshire, as a secretary for a spell and the experience obviously left a lasting impression on him, with Butler supposedly exacting revenge on his former employer through the work.

Butler, who served as an attendant at various country homes over the years, penned what was probably the most famous literary response to the tyranny of the Commonwealth. *Hudibras* mocked the Cromwellians and Presbyterianism through the chief character, Sir Hudibras, who is portrayed as dishonest, greedy and stupid.

Luke led the garrison at Newport Pagnell after Parliament took possession of it. It proved to be a very useful Parliamentarian stronghold for the remainder of the war.

The commander was a zealous Puritan who believed Newport Pagnell was in danger of suffering the same fate as Sodom and Gomorrah because of its sinful residents. Luke set up a programme of religious piety, which included prayer and Bible readings before the changing of the guard each morning. Traces of the fortifications can still be found in Bury Field.

Butler was in his 50s when he became famous through *Hudibras*, the first part appearing in 1663.

John Bunyan

The Pilgrim's Progress, arguably the greatest Christian book after the Bible, would not have been written if John Bunyan had not had a lucky – or perhaps providential – escape while in the service of Samuel Luke.

Bunyan was called up into the Parliamentary Army at the age of 16 and was based at the Newport Pagnell Garrison. In his autobiography, *Grace Abounding to the Chief of Sinners*, Bunyan recounts an occasion when a fellow soldier took his place on the watch and was shot in the head.

Though it is thought Bunyan did not see much action himself, his spell with the garrison, believed to have been from 1644 to at least 1646, certainly had a big influence in his later life. There is much military imagery in his work, such as in the allegorical epic, *The Holy War*. The writer served with zealous Puritans and his experience at Newport Pagnell affected his own spiritual journey, which is recorded in *Grace Abounding*.

Serene Newport Pagnell was once gripped by the Civil War.

Bunyan is more associated with Bedfordshire, but, as an itinerant preacher, he travelled extensively throughout his life and would have no doubt crossed the border into Buckinghamshire on numerous occasions. John Gibbs, the town's first non-conformist minister, was a good friend. Gibbs founded the Independent Meeting House, which stood on the site now occupied by the United Reformed Church.

William Cowper and John Newton

William Bull, another former minister of the town's Independent Meeting House, was a great friend of hymn-writers William Cowper and John Newton.

Cowper, in particular, would regularly visit Newport Pagnell from his Olney home.

Bull was 'a man of letters and of genius' himself, according to his more famous literary friend. The Newport Pagnell Academy, started by Bull to train non-conformist ministers, was the idea of Newton.

Some of Cowper's words can be found in the parish churchyard, the poet having written the epitaph to Thomas Hamilton. The tomb of Hamilton, a prominent lace merchant, is situated close to the town's almshouses.

William Cowper left his mark on a merchant's tomb.

George Fox

George Fox, the founder of the Quakers, revealed in his famous *Journal* that he 'stayed a while' in Newport Pagnell after – at the command of God – he had left his family in Leicestershire.

It is thought that Fox came to the town in 1644. He travelled widely, roaming around the country, wrestling with his soul, before embarking on his famous preaching mission. The much-persecuted Quakers particularly left their mark on Buckinghamshire, with the village of Jordans still considered something of a shrine to many followers today.

Samuel Pepys

Diarist Samuel Pepys visited Newport Pagnell in 1668 and described the Church of St Peter & St Paul as being 'like a cathedral'. Pepys is believed to have stayed at the Swan Hotel, now known as the Swan Revived. He travelled widely throughout Buckinghamshire.

Samuel Pepys stayed at the Swan Hotel.

MILTON KEYNES VILLAGE

William Wotton

The 'miracle' child, who went on to fight a war of words with the likes of Jonathan Swift, was one of the more unconventional rectors to serve Milton Keynes Village.

Linguist and theologian Wotton became the rector of All Saints' Church in 1693. He was a lover of women and wine, his behaviour often causing scandal among his parishioners. Buckinghamshire historian Browne Willis, of nearby Whaddon Hall, who was a student of Wotton and a great friend, described him as a debauched man who was likely to be undone by his own folly. He was perhaps right, as Wotton was forced to abandon his parish and move to Wales in 1714 under an assumed name in order to escape his creditors.

Unorthodox Wotton may have been, but he was also something of a genius. He was so advanced in his learning at the age of 11, that diarist John Evelyn used the word 'miracle' to describe him. Wotton was said to have been able to read Greek, Latin and Hebrew by the age of 5.

In literature, Wotton is remembered for his part in the debate between 'Ancients and Moderns', a serious cultural issue at the time. Wotton took the side of the contemporary writers and philosophers of the day, becoming one of the leading scholars in the 'modern' camp. He wrote *Reflections Upon Ancient and Modern Learning* in response to William Temple's essay on *Ancient and Modern Learning*, which opposed contemporary studies and sided with the ancient classical writers and philosophers.

Wotton's work prompted Swift, another in the 'ancient' camp, to pen *The Battle of the Books*. Swift also mocked Wotton in *A Tale of a Tub*.

Lewis Atterbury

Lewis Atterbury preceded William Wotton as the rector of Milton Keynes Village. He served All Saints' Church from 1657 until his untimely death in 1693. Atterbury's chief work was *Babylon's Downfall*, which appeared in 1691. It is a retrospective look at the 1688 Revolution, its sub-title, *England's Happy Deliverance from Popery and Slavery*, giving more than an indication of what the author thought of the event.

Atterbury, who is buried in the church, published numerous sermons before he drowned after falling from his horse into a brook close to his home. His two sons, Lewis Atterbury and Francis Atterbury, both also wrote sermons and other works. Francis later becoming a celebrated bishop.

WOOLSTONE

Weeden Butler

Weeden Butler, who used his pen to highlight the horrors of the slave trade, was the rector of Great Woolstone from 1816 until his death in 1831. Butler, little known today, translated *Zimao, the African*, an anti-slavery narrative which was published in 1800.

FENNY STRATFORD

Browne Willis

Historian and antiquary Browne Willis lies at rest in Fenny Stratford – for at least 364 days a year, at any rate. But even he could be forgiven for stirring on 11 November each year.

This is when the famous Fenny Poppers are fired. Browne Willis was himself responsible for the custom. The writer – one of Buckinghamshire's greatest local historians – built the Church of St Martin. His passion, apart from local history, was building and restoring churches. Browne Willis ordered a special service to be held on 11 November each year – St Martin's Day. This involved firing the Fenny Poppers – six pieces of ordnance – from a cannon in a nearby field in honour of his father and grandfather, Dr Thomas Willis, who died on November 11. A famous physician and writer of medical treatises, Thomas Willis also lived and died in St Martin's Lane in the parish of St Martin-in-the-Fields, providing Browne Willis with a further incentive to dedicate his new church to that particular saint.

Such was his generosity in building churches, that Browne Willis spent most of his money and was reduced to living a basic existence. He was often mistaken as a beggar in latter life. The author died at Whaddon Hall in 1760. His memorial in the church at Fenny Stratford also pays tribute to his grandfather. Only the chapel, where Browne Willis lies, remains of his original building.

Browne Willis was a prolific writer, responsible for some 100 volumes of handwritten manuscripts. His handwriting was so poor, it is said he himself had trouble reading it. He wrote a comprehensive history on Buckinghamshire, still considered to be the authoritative guide, as well as a number of ecclesiastical works.

The Fenny Poppers are still fired each year and the noise can be heard twelve miles away in Olney.

WHADDON

Edmund Spenser

Poet Edmund Spenser would probably have been a regular visitor to Whaddon Hall. The author of *The Faerie Queene* was, from 1580, secretary to Lord Grey of Wilton, Lord Deputy of Ireland and owner of the manor. Queen Elizabeth I was among the guests here and Spenser would also have come.

Buckinghamshire antiquary Browne Willis believed that Spenser did more than just visit. Browne Willis, who lived here for most of his life until his death in 1760, was of the opinion that Spenser wrote his greatest work within the shade of an ancient oak tree in the garden. Browne Willis cherished this tree because of its associations with one of literature's most celebrated writers.

St MARTIN'S CHURCH

HOME OF THE

FENNY POPPERS

'FENNY POPPER FAYRE'
Aylesbury Street
SUNDAY AUGUST 19TH

The Poppers will be on display here in the Church from 11.00 am

Above: *The Fenny Poppers are still fired each year.*

Right: *Browne Willis built the original St Martin's Church at Fenny Stratford.*

STONY STRATFORD

William Shakespeare

Stony Stratford, located on the old Roman road of Watling Street, was one of the most important coaching towns in England during the eighteenth century. Over the years, many would have spent at least a night here to break up their travels to and from London and the north.

William Shakespeare, in *Richard III*, informs us that Edward V, on the way to the capital to be crowned following his father's death, spent the night in the town. 'At Stony Stratford they do rest tonight,' the Lord Cardinal informs the Duchess of York.

A plaque at the former Rose & Crown Inn suggests that this is where the evil Duke of Gloucester, uncle and guardian to the young Prince Edward, 'captures' the uncrowned boy king, relaying him to the Tower, where, according to tradition, he and his brother were later murdered, the Duke taking the throne as Richard III.

Edward V resided at the former Rose & Crown, as the plaque and Shakespeare inform us.

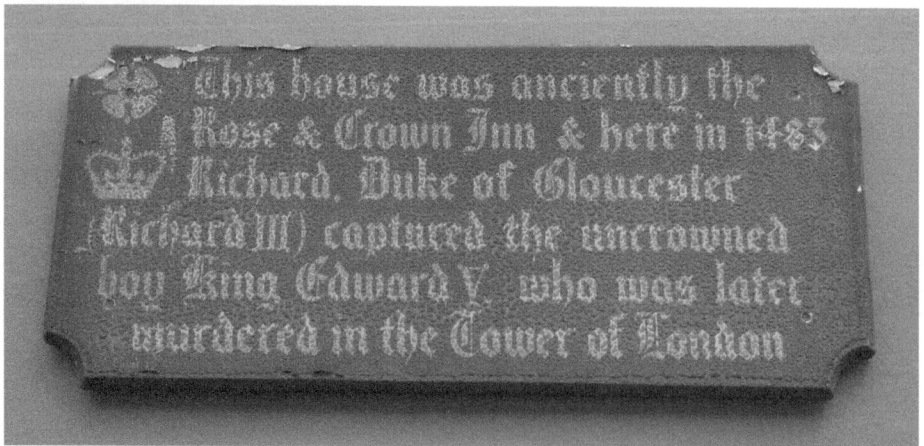

John Wesley

John Wesley, a frequent traveller throughout Buckinghamshire, preached under the elm tree in the market square on at least five occasions. Though a dynamic speaker, who drew large crowds, his message might not have been so well received in Stony Stratford. Wesley said of the town: 'Stony by nature, Stony by name.'

Wesley's remarkable life as an itinerant preacher and founder of Methodism is recorded in his own *Journal*, which consists of more than a million words, making it one of the most complete autobiographies ever published. Wesley also wrote religious tracts and treatises, as well as editing some of his brother Charles Wesley's hymns. He travelled throughout Britain, clocking up thousands of miles on horseback and went on preaching well into his 80s.

Little remains today of John Wesley's tree.

Samuel Johnson stayed at the Cock . . . and that's no 'cock and bull story'!

Samuel Johnson

The author of the English dictionary was another traveller who put up sticks for the night on at least one occasion, staying at the Cock Hotel. The term 'cock and bull story' originated at Stony Stratford, many travellers swapping 'tall' stories while residing at the two hostelries – The Cock and The Bull. Both still survive.

George Eliot

Fictitious characters have also travelled through Stony Stratford. In George Eliot's *Adam Bede*, Hetty Sorrel, in her attempt to find Arthur Donnithorne, embarks on a journey south to Windsor. Unsure of how to get there, she is given a list of places she must pass through, Stratford being one of them. Unfortunately, she first goes to Stratford-on-Avon by mistake. 'It was not till the fifth day that she got to Stony Stratford.' George Eliot knew the town well, coming on regular occasions to visit relatives here.

Charles Dickens

The famous Victorian novelist stayed in Stony Stratford on several occasions and was inspired by some of the town's more eccentric characters.

It is said that Mr Turveydrop in *Bleak House*, one of Dickens's most outrageous creations, was modelled on the dance teacher, Joseph Hambling, who had a school in Church Street.

Benjamin Holloway

Benjamin Holloway, the prominent Anglican divine and religious controversialist, was born in Stony Stratford at the end of the seventeenth century.

Holloway, also a respected scientist and fellow of the Royal Society, went on to become the rector of Waddesdon in 1726.

2

Buckingham and the Vale of Aylesbury

The Vale of Aylesbury – one of England's richest agricultural regions – stretches between two major towns.

To the north is Buckingham, a town that honours a novelist who captured, in a series of novels, a rural way of life that has been lost forever. To the south of this great expanse of flatland is Aylesbury itself, the new county town, fittingly represented by a radical writer and politician who was all for change and progress. And in between are some of the country's most isolated villages, churches and grand houses, where men and women of letters have left their mark.

BUCKINGHAM

Flora Thompson

Many writers are a little coy about revealing the inspiration for their fictional settings. Not Flora Thompson. The author of the semi-autobiographical *Lark Rise to Candleford* declared that Candleford was based on Buckingham, Brackley and Banbury, the latter two towns situated in Northamptonshire and Oxfordshire.

Flora was born at Juniper Hill in Oxfordshire and there is no doubt Lark Rise was based on her first home, the many skylarks in the area inspiring the name. The author wrote about her childhood memories, *Lark Rise to Candleford* being an account of a child growing up in the Oxfordshire, Northamptonshire and Buckinghamshire countryside. The work is an enduring portrayal of a world long vanished, a way of life where humble farm workers and craftsmen dominated the landscape and rural villages. Few works have better captured the decay of agricultural life in Victorian England.

Though Flora Thompson, née Timms, was an Oxfordshire girl, the Buckinghamshire border was close and she knew the county well. She visited Buckingham on a regular basis, as her father, a stonemason, had many relatives in the town. The Timms had long been associated with Buckingham.

Buckingham's Old Gaol Museum honours Flora Thompson.

Flora knew the Buckinghamshire villages between the county town and her home well, and these communities also became her inspiration, her own family and friends among those that led her pen in later life. Few authors have returned to their childhood so successfully. The book was written towards the end of the author's life, but the vivid descriptions of the countryside and people could fool the reader into thinking it was penned long before.

Flora, born in 1876, was a shy and quiet girl who liked nothing more than reading a book or exploring the countryside. Her school was situated at Cottisford, which was later immortalised as Fordlow in her greatest work. Flora would walk the mile or so to school with her beloved brother.

Flora left home at the age of 14 to work in the Post Office. Her first posting was at nearby Fringford and it is thought she may have also worked for a spell at Twyford, just over the border in Buckinghamshire, before eventually moving to Hampshire and later Devon, where she died in 1947.

Flora loved writing and wrote numerous stories, articles and poems, though the success of her sister also gave her much encouragement. Betty Timms published a popular children's book, *The Little Grey Men of the Moor*, in 1926.

Lark Rise to Candleford was not published until 1939 and was followed by *Over to Candleford* two years later. The final book of the trilogy was *Candleford Green*, which appeared in 1943. The author was living in Devon at the time, but her childhood surroundings were evidently never far from her mind.

The Old Gaol Museum in the centre of Buckingham has a permanent exhibition devoted to Flora Thompson, containing various memorabilia connected with the author, including her typewriter. Interest in *Lark Rise to Candleford* has increased over time, with a major BBC television drama based on the trilogy screened in 2008.

Browne Willis

The Old Gaol Museum in the centre of Buckingham was the product of historian and antiquary Browne Willis, who built it in 1748. An MP for Buckingham from 1705–8, Willis wrote the first history of the town and worked tirelessly for it throughout his life.

Diarist Samuel Pepys was among the many literary travellers to visit Buckingham. It was 'a good old town', according to the writer, when he came in 1668.

STOWE

Alexander Pope

Visitors to Stowe might agree with Alexander Pope when he wrote that the gardens were a 'work to wonder at'. Stowe was the most famous landscape garden in England in the eighteenth century and many words were inspired by it. Pope was not the only poet to express its charms in verse, while others set about penning whole books on the subject, as the country could not get enough of this British treasure.

Pope was not just a man of letters, but a keen gardener and, according to many, the greatest influence in the gardening revolution of the 1720s and '30s. His own creation at his Twickenham home also became much celebrated. Pope was responsible for the change in attitude towards nature and landscape. He believed gardening to be almost an art, a landscape painting.

The writer was a great friend of Lord Cobham, the owner of Stowe at the time, and was a regular visitor. In *Epistle to Burlington*, the poet refers to Cobham's creation as the model landscape garden. 'Nature shall join you; time shall make

The Temple of British Worthies.

it grow . . . A work to wonder at – perhaps a Stowe,' he wrote. Cobham was himself also the subject of another of Pope's epistles, while the poet is celebrated at Stowe. He is one of a number of literary figures represented in the Temple of British Worthies, a semi-circle of niches containing busts. John Milton, William Shakespeare, John Locke, Isaac Newton and Francis Bacon also figure. Pope himself chose the figures to grace the Temple of Ancient Virtue, the author Homer being among the greats celebrated here.

Pope was not the only literary visitor to Stowe. It became an entertainment venue for Lord Cobham's many distinguished friends.

Dramatist William Congreve spent many summers here and Cobham commemorated his wit via a statue of a monkey. Congreve's Monument is situated on an island in a lake. The poet James Thomson described 'the fair majestic paradise of Stowe' in *The Seasons*, while Celia Fiennes, Horace Walpole and Jonathan Swift were among the other guests.

Stowe House, the principal temple in the gardens, is now a school.

Above: *Alexander Pope is honoured in the Temple of British Worthies.*

Right: *The Temple of Ancient Virtue honours Homer.*

T.H. White taught at Stowe.

T.H. White

Novelist Terence Hanbury White was a schoolmaster at Stowe in the 1930s. The famous school became an inspiration for the children's novel *Mistress Masham's Repose*.

When White quit teaching to become a full-time writer, he moved to a gamekeeper's cottage on the estate. His own experiences in training a bird of prey here inspired the novel, *The Goshawk*, which was published in 1951.

White's other works include *The Sword in the Stone*, a much-loved children's tale, part of a sequence of novels collected under the name *The Once and Future King*, which inspired the famous Broadway musical, *Camelot*.

WATER STRATFORD

John Mason

The unassuming village of Water Stratford would not be the most obvious location for the Second Coming, even if God – as Olney hymn-writer William Cowper declared – 'moves in a mysterious way'.

However, John Mason, himself a hymn-writer and rector here for some twenty years at the end of the seventeenth century, sincerely believed Water Stratford was the place where Christ would return to bring judgement on his people and that this day was near. He was not the only one either. Many fell under his spell, selling their properties to set up home in the village, living in barns and tents. Noisy meetings ensued, with dancing and singing, day and night, as the makeshift

Rector John Mason caused quite a stir at the Church of St Giles.

community waited for the Lord's return. Mason's followers believed Water Stratford would be the only place to survive the wrath of God.

Mason died at the height of the activities at Water Stratford, having earlier declared that he himself, like Christ, would rise three days after his death. His disciples believed it too and refused to accept he was 'dead', even when the three days had elapsed. Mason's successor had the grave opened in a futile bid to convince people that this was the case, but the community survived for many more years to come.

It is not known exactly when Mason turned from being a devout and celebrated hymn-writer to a fanatic Adventist. He was certainly a popular man in his early days, even if he did possess strong Calvinist views. Preacher and writer Richard Baxter referred to him as 'the glory of the Church of England'.

Mason's hymns, published in 1683, formed one of the first compositions in English hymnody and are said to have influenced hymn-writer Charles Wesley.

Mason served the Church of St Giles from 1674 until his death in 1694 and had earlier been the vicar of Stantonbury. Sadly, his latter life now overshadows his many hymns, such as *How Shall I Sing that Majesty*, which were among the earliest in the Church of England.

Scholar Joseph Bosworth, who is remembered for his *Dictionary of the Anglo-Saxon Language*, was the rector of Water Stratford for a spell in the second half of the nineteenth century, having earlier served the parish of Little Horwood.

GAWCOTT

George Gilbert Scott

It is not surprising churches were to play a big part in the life of George Gilbert Scott. The famous architect was born the son of a clergyman and, though he did not follow his father into the Church, he did at least go on to build numerous places of worship.

Scott, the leading architect of the Gothic Revival, shared his father's passion for architecture from an early age. Scott Senior was himself an amateur architect and built the parsonage at Gawcott in which George Gilbert was born in 1811. He also rebuilt Holy Trinity Church, in which he served.

Most of the Scott family were employed within the Church, but, throughout the county, and at Gawcott in particular, they were not always popular, the parishioners often taking issue with their leanings towards the Evangelical wing of the Church of England. George Gilbert Scott was not the only famous member of the family. His grandfather was clergyman Thomas Scott, the biblical commentator who served Olney and spent the final years of his life in the village of Aston Sandford, near Haddenham.

It is with bricks and mortar that George Gilbert Scott gained fame, but he, like his grandfather, also took up his pen. Scott wrote numerous books, articles and reports on ancient buildings, particularly cathedrals and churches. It is amazing he found time to write – he was responsible for hundreds of new buildings throughout the country – but Scott himself said 'pretty well all that I write is the product of my travelling hours'. *A Plea for the Faithful Restoration of our Ancient Churches* was typical of his desire to see sensitivity when dealing with ancient buildings, but he often had to forego his own principles for practical reasons. *Gleanings from Westminster Abbey* proved Scott was also a great scholar and highlighted his love for medieval architecture, while *Personal and Professional Recollections* is an interesting account of his own life, including his early years in Gawcott as a boy. It was one of the first autobiographies of an architect to be published.

Scott was initially educated at home by his father before attending a prep school run by a clergyman-uncle in Latimer, near Chesham, in 1826. The following year he moved to London to begin his career as an architect, eventually becoming one of the country's most celebrated figures. Many churches in Buckinghamshire are the work of Scott. Ironically, it is said Holy Trinity Church – the work of his father – did not impress him.

Edward Gibbon

Lenborough House, on the outskirts of Gawcott, once belonged to Edward Gibbon, one of the country's most celebrated historians.

But Gibbon, famous for *The History of the Decline and Fall of the Roman Empire*, was anxious to get rid of the manor. Following his father's death in 1770, the writer was left with a number of financial problems to clear up. He made many attempts to sell the Lenborough estate in order to fund the expensive and fashionable life he led in the capital. Gibbon's grandfather, a successful businessman, acquired the manor in 1718. The historian actually pulled most of the house down before it left the family.

Holy Trinity Church, Gawcott, played a big part in the life of George Gilbert Scott.

HILLESDEN

William Denton

The Church of All Saints at Hillesden is the resting place of William Denton, a political writer and physician to Charles I and II.

Though little remembered today, Denton was a prominent member of the royal household and his views held much sway. The scribe, an Anglican, held strong anti-Papist beliefs, but his later works, in particular, advocated religious tolerance. He wrote numerous treatises on matters concerning the power of the monarchy and the Church.

Denton, who was born at Stowe, was baptised at Hillesden in 1605 and laid to rest here following his death in London in 1691. The Dentons were former owners of the manor and All Saints' Church contains several family monuments.

ADSTOCK

A number of minor authors have associations with Adstock. Luke Heslop, a political and economic writer, was a former rector at the end of the eighteenth and beginning of the nineteenth centuries.

William Denton is buried at Hillesden Church.

Scholar and political writer Charles Neate was born here in 1806, while Robert Sharrock, whose father also held the rectorship for a spell, lived in the village. Sharrock Junior, who himself became the rector of nearby Great Horwood in the 1660s, was baptised at Drayton Parslow, another of his father's former rectorships. Sharrock was a celebrated botanist and the author of *The History of the Propagation and Improvement of Vegetables*.

Walter Scott

Walter Scott drew on a famous family associated with the county for his novel *Peveril of the Peak*.

The Peverels were Derbyshire landowners, but also held a number of estates in Buckinghamshire, including Adstock and, most notably, Hartwell near Aylesbury.

Because of William Peverel's role in the poisoning of Ranulf, Earl of Chester, he was forced to flee the country and his land at Adstock was given to the Avenels, a name that appears in two other Scott novels – *The Monastery* and *The Abbot*. *Peveril of the Peak* features many real-life characters, including writer George Villiers, 2nd Duke of Buckingham.

Sarah Fyge Egerton

Poet Sarah Fyge Egerton can claim to be one of the earliest feminists – and certainly one of the youngest.

She penned *The Female Advocate*, a polemical reply to an attack on women, when she was just 14 years old. The work was published a couple of years later, in 1686, without her consent. Her father, a Winslow landowner, was not impressed and packed her off to relatives.

Little is known about Sarah's personal life, but it is clear from her work that she was an ardent supporter of women's rights. *The Female Advocate*, a satire in verse, boldly declared that women were, in fact, superior to men.

The author penned numerous tracts and poems. Her second husband was Thomas Egerton, the rector of Adstock, though it was thought to be an unhappy marriage. The Egertons have long been associated with the village.

GREAT HORWOOD

Joseph Spence

Joseph Spence, the clergyman anecdotist and great friend of Alexander Pope, became the rector of Great Horwood in 1742.

Though it is thought he did not actually reside in the village, he made regular visits to tend to the needs of his parishioners and his garden. Like Pope, Spence was a keen gardener and planted extensively at Great Horwood.

Spence became the friend of Pope following the publication of *Essay on Pope's Odyssey* in 1726, in which he defended the writer. He took notes of his many conversations with Pope and other literary friends, publishing their anecdotes, for which he is now chiefly remembered.

NEWTON LONGVILLE

William Grocyn

Humanist William Grocyn became the rector of Newton Longville in 1479. He is chiefly remembered as the man who first introduced the study of Greek to Oxford University and for his friendship with fellow humanists, Desiderius Erasmus and Thomas More.

Grocyn held various ecclesiastical offices and was invited to preach at St Paul's when humanist John Colet became its dean. Few of his literary works have survived, one exception being a Latin epigram on a lady throwing a snowball.

STEWKLEY

Emmeline Pankhurst

Stewkley is a good place to hide. It is reputed to be the second longest village in England. Its high street, almost two miles long, is more continuously populated than Combe Martin in Devon, which claims to be the longest.

Ivy Lane is just one road off the high street in Stewkley and here, in a red-brick cottage, Emmeline Pankhurst, a leading women's rights activist, took refuge on occasions just before the First World War. She used the cottage as a country residence and hideaway when things got out of hand in the capital. The movement had become more militant at this time and Emmeline was under constant threat of arrest. She and her daughters were among the many to pen accounts of the women's suffrage movement.

Emmeline Pankhurst took refuge in this Stewkley cottage.

SWANBOURNE

Elizabeth Fremantle

The village of Swanbourne could hardly be further from the sea, but its development owes much to a family with a strong naval tradition.

Diarist Elizabeth 'Betsey' Fremantle, née Wynne, settled here with her seafaring husband at the end of the eighteenth century, and the family still own the manor.

Betsey's literary claim to fame is the fascinating *Wynne Diaries*, accounts she and her sisters gave of their eventful lives between 1789 and 1820. Betsey was the chief contributor.

Her story was one worthy of being published. She spent her upbringing travelling in Europe, her father being a carefree rogue and friend of Casanova. When the French invaded Italy in 1796, the family sought protection from the British fleet and boarded a ship captained by Thomas Fremantle, one of Lord Nelson's faithful companions. Betsey, still a teenager, fell in love with the captain and won his heart, the couple marrying in Naples in 1797 at the home of Emma Hamilton, who later became the famous mistress of Nelson.

It is thought that Betsey was the recipient of the first words Nelson wrote with his left hand, after losing his right arm. Her husband had also been hit in the arm during the ill-fated battle with the Spanish, but his limb was saved, Betsey helping to nurse both seamen. Nelson wrote on the following day: 'God bless you and Fremantle.'

On the couple's return to England, they settled in rural Buckinghamshire, bringing up a large family, one of whom became a famous MP, while another embarked on a life at sea and had the honour of Fremantle in Western Australia

The village pub honours diarist Betsey Wynne.

being named after him. Thomas Fremantle, meanwhile, went on to fight alongside Nelson at the Battle of Trafalgar.

Betsey continued to write her diaries in Swanbourne, something she had started as a child. She was hugely popular in the village and remains so. A pub, The Betsey Wynne, is named in her honour. The diaries, unlike many of the age, were more social than political. Following her adventures on the high seas, the entries became preoccupied with domestic trivialities, but give a valuable insight into the manners of the day and high-society living.

Many local places feature, including Wotton House near Aylesbury, home of the Grenvilles, and Stowe, two of the county's finest properties.

WINSLOW

Benjamin Keach

A literary secret lies within a tiny chapel hidden behind Winslow's market square.

Keach's Meeting House, one of the country's first places of worship for non-conformists, attracts many to the town. However, few who marvel at this delightful relic from a troubled era know how much Baptist pastor Benjamin Keach suffered because of his pen.

Keach, who was born at Stoke Hammond, was a zealous preacher who was not afraid to put his radical views into print. He was a voluminous writer of theological works and poems. *The Child's Instructor*, which appeared in 1664, caused outrage. The book of introduction for children did not conform to Church of England doctrine and was considered to be heresy. Keach was against child baptism, believing only adults could make a decision to follow God.

The author was briefly imprisoned, fined and put in the pillory for his troubles. His 'seditious' book was publicly burned in Winslow.

The meeting house's isolated location is not a coincidence. The dissenters suffered much and their personal well-being, as Keach discovered, was often under threat.

CLAYDON HOUSE

Frances Parthenope Verney and Florence Nightingale

A novelist has perhaps a better chance of earning lasting fame than a humble nurse.

Visitors to the National Trust's Claydon House at Middle Claydon discover this is not always the case, however. Few have heard of Frances Parthenope Verney, a former owner and woman of letters, but few have *not* heard of her sister – Florence Nightingale.

Frances penned novels, now almost forgotten, and also compiled *Memoirs of the Verney Family*, an interesting insight into seventeenth-century manners and country living.

The Verneys have long been associated with Claydon House. Frances, who came to Middle Claydon following her marriage to MP Harry Verney, was not keen on

Benjamin Keach's Meeting House.

Florence Nightingale came to Claydon House.

Florence becoming a nurse and sided with their mother in actively discouraging her from taking that road. Florence was a regular visitor to Claydon House, usually staying with her sister whenever she returned to England.

Florence Nightingale was a writer herself, penning numerous works on her chosen profession, including the best-selling *Notes on Nursing*. She became the inspiration for a number of other writers. Henry Wadsworth Longfellow wrote perhaps the most famous poem on this great British heroine.

STEEPLE CLAYDON

Thomas Chaloner

Placid rural Buckinghamshire could not have been a bigger contrast to the war-ravaged high seas experienced by Thomas Chaloner in his early life.

The soldier, diplomat and poet acquired a number of estates during his years of service, including Steeple Claydon in 1557.

Chaloner wrote throughout his life and was much admired by his contemporaries. He penned Latin verses and pastoral poems, as well as epigrams and epitaphs. He was the first English translator of Desiderius Erasmus's *The Praise of Folly* and contributed the tragedy of Richard II in *A Mirror for Magistrates*, a collection of didactic poems that highlighted the instability of fortune, focusing on the downfall of prominent men and punishment of the wicked.

Despite his literary achievements, it is Chaloner's own life for which he is chiefly remembered, and he became the inspiration for many fellow writers. Richard Hakluyt recalls Chaloner's thrilling adventures at sea in *Voyages*. Chaloner was just 19 when he was shipwrecked off the coast of Africa. Hakluyt tells us that Chaloner 'escaped most wonderfully with his life' by clinging to a cable with his teeth after becoming too exhausted to carry on swimming.

Chaloner, who was born in 1521, fought many wars and was knighted on the field of battle. He served various monarchs during one of the most dangerous periods of English history. Though Steeple Claydon became one of his homes, most of his latter life was spent abroad before his death in 1565.

TWYFORD

Agnes Wenman

The church at Twyford is the resting place of Agnes Wenman. Agnes, a strong Catholic, is remembered for a translation of the most famous work of John Zonaras. His epic history of the world begins at the Creation and ends in the twelfth century.

Agnes was married to the first Viscount Wenman, both of whom fell under suspicion of being involved in the Gunpowder Plot. The Wenmans, whose principal seat was at Thame Park, also had a mansion at Twyford, though it no longer exists.

GRENDON UNDERWOOD

William Shakespeare

It is highly likely William Shakespeare knew Buckinghamshire very well. He would have had to pass through the county when travelling between London and his native Warwickshire, and it is thought that he regularly chose to break his journey at Grendon Underwood. The village is close to Bernwood Forest, once a favourite haunt of gypsies and strolling players like Shakespeare, who would camp here on their way to and from the capital.

It is said Shakespeare frequented the Ship Inn, but, on one occasion, he ended up sleeping in the church porch. Two conscientious Grendon constables believed him to be a vagrant and had the scribe arrested. The church chest was opened, but nothing had been stolen and Shakespeare was eventually released. Presumably, the Bard thought the incident 'much ado about nothing' and the two keepers of the law were immortalised as Dogberry and Verges in his famous play.

Most of what we know about Shakespeare and his adventures in Grendon Underwood comes from the pen of antiquary John Aubrey. The historian claimed to have met one of the two constables who had arrested the Bard, when he came to the village many years after the death of Shakespeare. Aubrey was not the only one to write on the subject, however, and there have been many versions of the same story.

The Ship Inn, now Shakespeare House, is close to St Leonard's Church. It has also been suggested that Shakespeare stayed in an attic room overlooking the forest and penned *A Midsummer Night's Dream* here. How true this is would be difficult to say, as much about England's greatest writer remains a mystery, but it certainly

Shakespeare House in Grendon Underwood.

*St Leonard's Church, where
the Bard once slept.*

conjures up a lovely image: the playwright looking out of his window towards the forest, imagining the king and queen of the fairies, later immortalised as Oberon and Titania, twinkling in the moonlight.

LUDGERSHALL

John Wycliffe

Bible translator and theologian John Wycliffe had the best of both worlds in Ludgershall: he could serve God here, but also continue his studies.

Wycliffe became the rector of St Mary's Church in 1368, leaving his ministry in Lincolnshire for one closer to Oxford. The village is close to the Oxfordshire border and Wycliffe, who had earlier studied at Oxford University, was able to continue with his studies there, while also tending to the needs of his parishioners. It is thought that he lived in the city, his Ludgershall rectorship being a non-residential one. Within six years, Wycliffe had moved to Lutterworth in Leicestershire and retained that post until his death.

Wycliffe played a major role in the reformation of religion. He attacked Rome's control over the Church of England and its many practices. Indulgent and wealthy priests became a target for his pen, and he boldly declared that they had no power to absolve sins.

Wycliffe wrote numerous tracts, but is best remembered for his role in the first complete English translation of the Bible. Buckinghamshire became a stronghold for Wycliffe's followers, of which many suffered for their beliefs, notably at Amersham.

BOARSTALL

Henry Wade

Henry Wade – also known as Henry Lancelot Aubrey-Fletcher – inherited Boarstall Tower in the twentieth century. Wade was the author of popular crime novels, writing during the Golden Age of detective fiction in the 1920s and '30s, his most famous creation being Inspector John Poole of Scotland Yard. He wrote some twenty detective novels and short stories.

The Aubreys have long been associated with Boarstall Manor and lived here until moving to the nearby village of Chilton, which became Henry Lancelot Aubrey-Fletcher's home. Boarstall Tower is all that remains of the manor house and is now in the care of the National Trust.

Anthony à Wood

Antiquary Anthony à Wood visited Boarstall during one of the most troubled times in its history. Wood, a schoolboy at nearby Thame, came on a number of occasions during the Civil War when the property was the object of several skirmishes between the Royalists and Parliamentarians, experiences he later set down in print.

Boarstall House was owned by the Denhams (or Dynhams) at the time, Lady Penelope living here throughout the troubles. Some historians have suggested a link with Cavalier poet John Denham, who was the owner of a number of estates in the south-east of England, including Horsenden, near Princes Risborough.

Denham, whose chief residence was at Egham in Surrey, was greatly admired by his peers, but he appeared to have had a low opinion of himself as a man of verse. He famously helped to secure a pardon for fellow scribe and Puritan opponent George Wither, who was imprisoned in the Tower on a charge of sedition, Denham believing that while Wither lived, he himself would not be the worst poet in England!

Novelist Henry Wade inherited Boarstall Tower.

OAKLEY

James Tyrrell and John Locke

It is easy to imagine James Tyrrell and John Locke, two great thinkers of the day, bouncing ideas of each other at the Oakley home of the former.

The philosophical works of Tyrrell, in his day, were considered more influential than those of his close friend, but it is Locke who has gained lasting fame. Locke stayed with Tyrrell at Oakley for long periods during the early 1680s and penned part of *Two Treatises of Government* here. When the work appeared, Tyrrell was the only living author named in it and many believed it to be from his pen.

Tyrrell was born in London and moved to Oakley following his marriage in 1670. He had met Locke at Oxford and the two remained close friends, sharing controversial views on politics and religion.

Tyrrell was not just a philosopher, but a notable political historian. He penned *The General History of England*, a defence of English ancient constitution.

The Tyrrells were long-time lords of the manor and there are many family memorials in the parish church at Oakley, including a mural to James, who eventually sold the estate to live at Shotover House, near Oxford, the family's other residence. Tyrrell died at Shotover in 1718 but is buried in the church at Oakley. His monument in the church highlights his literary achievements and adds that he was 'a man of rare integrity, gravity and wisdom [who] had never polished himself out of his Sincerity, nor refined his Behaviour to the prejudice of his Virtue'.

Tyrrell's mother was the daughter of Bible chronologist James Ussher, who, through his work, determined that the Creation took place on 23 October 4004 BC. Tyrrell's literary output includes works on his famous grandfather.

WORMINGHALL

Henry King

Poet Henry King began his eventful life in the village of Worminghall, close to the Oxfordshire border. He followed in the footsteps of his father in becoming a bishop and gained fame for his many elegies. Close friends, John Donne (who was ordained by King's father), and Ben Jonson were among his subjects, though an elegy on his wife is considered to be his best work.

King became Bishop of Chichester, but was deprived of his bishopric during the Civil War, only to be reinstated at the Restoration. He was a firm opponent of Puritanism and a resolute preacher.

Little is known about King's early life, though records show he was baptised in Worminghall in January 1592 and attended Thame Grammar School.

Memorials to the King family can be found in the parish church. The village almshouses are also named in honour of the author. His son, carrying out his father's dying wish to help the poor, built them.

J.R.R. Tolkien mentions Worminghall in his fable *Farmer Giles of Ham*. The title character is the Lord of Thame and Count of Worminghall.

The village almshouses are named after Henry King.

ICKFORD

William Joyner

Dramatist William Joyner has faded into obscurity – and it seems his fame started to decline even during his own lifetime. He ended his days in Buckinghamshire and Oxfordshire a lonely and withdrawn figure. Extremely devout and pious, Joyner is said to have dressed like a labourer and lived in humble lodgings, shunning the limelight for an obscure existence.

Joyner, who changed his name to Lyde, is best known for the tragedy *The Roman Empress*, which appeared in 1671. He also wrote poems in Latin and English.

After studying at Thame and Oxford, Joyner became a Catholic and supported the Royalist cause during the Civil War. He spent a spell in the service of Queen Henrietta Maria. It is thought he moved to Ickford in the late 1670s, taking up residence at the home of sister Mary Phillips, where he continued his devout existence. By 1686, he was living in Wales, where he published a biography on Cardinal Reginald Pole, but Joyner returned to Ickford two years later, before seemingly spending his final poverty-stricken days in the village of Brill and at a house in Oxford.

William Joyner was the great uncle of Thomas Phillips, who is remembered for an even more famous biography on Cardinal Reginald Pole. Phillips was born at Ickford in 1708 and *The History of the Life of Reginald Pole* was published in the 1760s.

Calybute Downing, a respected theologian who wrote much on Church politics, became the rector of Ickford in 1632, following a spell at Quainton. Downing was replaced by Gilbert Sheldon four years later. Sheldon, who went on to become Archbishop of Canterbury and a great defender of the Church of England, published sermons and other theological works, but is best known for funding the building of the distinctive Sheldonian Theatre in Oxford.

WOTTON UNDERWOOD

Thomas Grenville

Many important people have graced Wotton House – the principal seat of the Grenvilles – over the years.

Though the family is more associated with politics than literature (it has produced two British prime ministers), one of its members can certainly be described as a man of letters, even if he did not actually pen them himself.

Thomas Grenville, son of the prime minister George and brother of the prime minister William, also became a politician, but is remembered as arguably the country's greatest bibliophile. Grenville had an extensive knowledge of literature and spent some fifty years building up his remarkable library. He bequeathed about 16,000 works to the British Museum, and the collection – containing many rare first editions – is thought to have been worth about £50,000, even then. Grenville had a wide circle of literary friends, none closer than poet Richard Brinsley Sheridan.

Wotton House, home of the Grenvilles.

WADDESDON MANOR

Virginia Woolf

Most of the great houses of Buckinghamshire have entertained some of the leading literary lights of the day, but Waddesdon Manor can probably claim to have entertained them all.

Virginia Woolf leads a strong cast of women and men of letters who came to the most famous home of the Rothschild family. A relative of husband Leonard Woolf was a former chatelaine here. In fact, anyone who was anyone attended the grand opening of Waddesdon Manor towards the end of the nineteenth century. Everyone wanted an invitation.

Weekend house parties became legendary. Henry James and Guy de Maupassant were among the many to delight in the extravagance of Waddesdon Manor. The house, built by Baron Ferdinand de Rothschild to display his art treasures and entertain the rich and famous, is now in the hands of the National Trust.

QUAINTON

Richard Brett

Linguist Richard Brett was a perfect choice to become one of the forty-seven men who worked on the translation of the *Authorised Version of the Bible* for King James in the early seventeenth century.

Brett, who was the rector of Quainton from 1595 until his death in 1637, was renowned for his piety and his incredible language skills, and he was fluent in numerous languages. Brett is buried at the church he served in Quainton and there is a monument to his memory.

Calybute Downing, the Puritan divine, married the daughter of the rector Richard Brett at Quainton in 1627. Downing came to the village as the curate the year before and went on to become the rector of Ickford on the Buckinghamshire–Oxfordshire border in 1632. Downing wrote on matters concerning the Church, State and monarchy during one of the most troubled times in English history.

George Lipscomb

Local historian and antiquary George Lipscomb was born at Magpie Cottage in 1773.

He devoted the best years of his life to producing what is arguably the definitive history of Buckinghamshire, but died as it was being printed.

Lipscomb attended schools in Quainton and Aylesbury, before moving to the Midlands to continue a successful medical career. He eventually returned to the county, moving to Whitchurch to practise medicine.

Lipscomb also produced medical writings, novels and a variety of other works, but will forever be remembered as the author of the voluminous *The History and Antiquities of the County of Buckingham*.

Magpie Cottage, the birthplace of George Lipscomb.

John Betjeman

Poet John Betjeman worked hard to preserve the beauty of the county and was horrified by the Metropolitan Railway's plan to make Quainton, as the author himself put it, the 'Crewe of Buckinghamshire'. However, it is only steam trains that rule here now, the Buckinghamshire Railway Centre being a popular tourist attraction.

NORTH MARSTON

John Heywood

Dramatist John Heywood was one of a number of writers to immortalise a North Marston rector in print.

John Schorne, who appears in the work of Heywood, became one of the most popular saints in pre-Reformation England. He helped put North Marston on the map when he served the parish at the end of the thirteenth and beginning of the fourteenth centuries. Pilgrims flocked to the village when Schorne, during a great drought, struck the earth with his staff, prompting a spring to appear. It was said that the water had healing properties and thousands came to North Marston in a bid to cure their ailments.

Schorne also gained fame for supposedly catching the Devil and placing him in a boot so that he could do no harm. It is believed the idea of a jack-in-the-box may have originated from the tale; the jack, grinning like an imp, constantly popping up and being forced back down.

Pilgrimages to Christian sites were common during this era – and big business, as Geoffrey Chaucer's *The Canterbury Tales* highlights. However, many humanists criticised the ever-increasing claims of miraculous powers, and the commercial gains that many made from it. The question of dubious veneration comes under scrutiny in Heywood's *The Four PP*, in which the Palmer boasts about his numerous visits to the shrines of saints, his inventory including many sites of questionable foundation. Heywood's farce, *Johan Johan*, contains a character named Sir John the Priest.

WHITCHURCH

Jan Struther

Few writers can claim to have influenced the course of war. Jan Struther, the pen name of Joyce Anstruther, was one of them. She was responsible for the novel *Mrs Miniver*, which became a successful Hollywood film. The work, about an ordinary British family, hastened America's entry into the Second World War according to President Franklin D. Roosevelt, while Winston Churchill declared it did more for the Allies than a flotilla of battleships. Even the Nazi Joseph Goebbels conceded it was an exemplary piece of propaganda.

Peter Fleming of *The Times* challenged Jan to create her most famous character. He told her to write about 'an ordinary sort of woman, who leads an ordinary sort of life – rather like yourself'. *Mrs Miniver* first appeared in *The Times* as a series of anonymous articles in 1937. The pieces about modern middle-class life were published once a fortnight for two years, before being collected to form the book, which finally revealed the author's identity. Over the Atlantic, the book topped the best-selling charts, as later did the film, doing much to influence people's attitudes to a Britain threatened by Nazi invasion. The propagandists had long striven to make the Americans understand the war. *Mrs Miniver*, published in the United States in 1940, succeeded where they had failed, with no obvious effort.

Mrs Miniver was a devoted housewife and mother, whose way of life was under threat. The work helped the Americans to comprehend why Britain had gone to war. They could now see what they were fighting for – a way of life, an England of village flower shows and cream teas. The American people were no longer detached from the reality, their views transformed by a rose-coloured portrayal of rural middle-class life in Britain.

During the height of Mrs Miniver's fame, Jan toured the United States as an unofficial British ambassador. The public often confused the family of Mrs Miniver with Jan's own family, such was the realism of the characters. Her sketches of family life were deceptively simple, but captivated a generation.

The author also wrote poems and hymns, including *When a Knight Won His Spurs* and *Lord of All Hopefulness*.

Jan was born in London in 1901 and spent her early childhood in the capital and at Whitchurch House in Oving Road, the family's country home from 1904–11. When her parents separated, her father remained in Whitchurch, living alone at Old Court House, a smaller property. Jan continued to visit him there and enjoyed many happy days, the two sharing a love for hunting. Jan's father went everywhere by

Whitchurch House, home of Jan Struther.

horse – he never owned a car – but was sadly killed in 1926 after being knocked off his mount by a double-decker bus.

Though Jan died in America, her ashes were flown home and buried in the churchyard at Whitchurch.

Winston Churchill

The Firs, a house opposite the White Swan, is known locally as 'Winston Churchill's Toyshop'. Churchill, a writer as well as a prime minister, came to the Firs during the Second World War when it was used as a secret MoD department. Weapons were made and tested here.

HARDWICK

Thomas Wood

The nephew of antiquary Anthony à Wood became the rector of the Church of St Mary in 1704. Thomas Wood was a celebrated lawyer, but, like his uncle, was also a prolific writer. He even picked up his pen to defend his more famous member of the family, when Anthony was gaining much criticism throughout the literary world.

Thomas wrote most of his legal works at Hardwick and died here in 1722. He is best remembered for *An Institute of the Laws of England*, the leading work on English law for many years.

WEEDON

George Nugent Grenville (Baron Nugent)

'Lilies' was the home of writer and politician George Nugent Grenville (Baron Nugent). He wrote on a wide range of subjects and delighted in the society of more illustrious writers than himself. Many distinguished visitors, including Charles Dickens and Robert Browning, are said to have planted trees in the grounds of the estate.

Nugent created a 'circle of friends', the trees accompanied by stone seats with the names of his contemporaries carved onto each. A Latin inscription expressed the host's hope that the friends would meet there often.

John Wesley

Preacher John Wesley, a prolific writer and the founder of Methodism, is said to have addressed a crowd from a mound near the crossroads in Weedon. Ironically, the name 'Weedon' actually means 'a place of heathen worship'. The village was the first place in the county licensed for Methodist services.

'Lilies' has welcomed many literary guests.

WING

William Dodd

William Dodd, a former vicar of Wing, was blissfully unaware of his fate when he published the sermon, *The Frequency of Capital Punishments Inconsistent with Justice, Sound Policy and Religion*. A few years later he was to experience the hangman's noose for himself.

Dodd was a popular English divine who moved in royal circles, but his expenses were greater than his income and he fell heavily into debt as he battled to sustain his extravagant lifestyle. In an attempt to clear his debts, Dodd dabbled in forgery and was eventually hanged for the crime at Tyburn in 1777.

Samuel Johnson was among those who picked up his pen to try to save this unfortunate clergyman from the gallows. He wrote eloquent letters pleading for mercy, but his efforts, as well as a massive publicity campaign, fell on deaf ears.

Dodd was a respected scholar who penned a variety of works, including a novel, poetry, theological tracts, sermons and a commentary on the Bible. His most famous work is *The Beauties of Shakespeare*, a collection of quotations.

Dodd served All Saints' Church for a few years before his untimely demise.

John Betjeman

John Betjeman was particularly fond of exploring Buckinghamshire's churches. He called All Saints' Church in Wing 'the finest and most important Saxon church in England'.

Betjeman did not just write about the county, but also did his bit to help retain its beauty. Wing was the site of a proposed airport in the 1970s and the poet made his views on the subject quite clear, penning a piece to aid the ultimately successful Wing Airport Resistance Association. Betjeman wrote: 'For who'd use a footpath to Quainton or Brill, when a jet can convey you so fast to Brazil?'

MENTMORE

Anthony Trollope

Novelist Anthony Trollope was one of many to accept the hospitality of Mayer Amschel de Rothschild, better known as the Baron. The two men shared a passion for hunting and Trollope took up the opportunity to enjoy the Baron's superb facilities at Mentmore.

Trollope, best known for his Barsetshire novels, said he loved hunting 'with an affection which I cannot myself fathom'. He took up the 'sport' when he moved to Ireland, and later became a regular of the Essex hunt when living at Waltham Cross on the Hertfordshire–Essex border. He declared in his autobiography: 'Nothing has ever been allowed to stand in the way of hunting.'

The Baron built the splendid Mentmore Towers in the early 1850s. The chief attraction of the estate was the fact it was set in the heart of fine hunting country. Trollope and many others took full advantage of the wide pastures of Aylesbury Vale.

Nearby Ascott House was also later rebuilt as a hunting box and is one of many fine Rothschild properties still dominating this part of the world, Waddesdon Manor being the most famous. The Baron's hunts, which sometimes included his famous breakfasts of champagne, brandy and sherry, took place throughout the Vale of Aylesbury.

The Baron established a stud farm on the Mentmore estate, land that also took in the hamlets of Crafton and Ledburn. The Hare & Hounds inn at Ledburn highlights the impact hunting had on the area. It was a former hostel for stable lads.

The Baron entertained greatly at Mentmore Towers, an extravagant property fit for any party.

HULCOTT

The Brontës

The Revd William Morgan, who served the Church of All Saints in Hulcott for a spell during the nineteenth century, could claim a part in the success of the world's most famous literary family. If he had not introduced a certain Patrick Brontë to Maria Branwell, there would have been no Charlotte, Emily, Anne and Branwell.

Morgan and Brontë were young curates together in Yorkshire and Morgan invited Brontë to the house of his future wife, Jane Fennell, the daughter of a local headmaster. It was on this occasion that Brontë first set eyes on Jane's cousin, Maria, who was to become his wife and mother to the famous novelists. This led to a double wedding, with the grooms conducting each other's ceremony. Unfortunately, Morgan came to Hulcott in 1851 without Jane. She had died before he settled here and he had remarried by this time.

Morgan was a critic and publisher of some of Patrick Brontë's early poetry.

Anthony Trollope came to Mentmore.

QUARRENDON

Walter Scott

A Quarrendon knight became the inspiration for one of Walter Scott's most famous characters. Henry Lee inspired the chief character of the same name in *Woodstock*, Scott's historical novel set during the Civil War. In the book, Lee is a Royalist and serves the monarchy against the Parliamentarians.

The real Lee – the Lees of Quarrendon were an ancient family – came to prominence in the previous century, serving Elizabeth I, and becoming the Queen's Champion. During a tournament, he made a vow of chivalry that he would, on the anniversary of her accession to the throne, maintain her honour against all-comers. Lee was lieutenant of Woodstock Park, which is situated over the border in Oxfordshire. The novel, as the title suggests, is also set at Woodstock.

Lee had a number of estates in both Buckinghamshire and Oxfordshire. The Lee family mansion at Quarrendon, on the outskirts of Aylesbury, no longer exists.

AYLESBURY

John Wilkes

Modern tabloids have much to thank people like John Wilkes for. The radical reformer and apostle of liberty fought long and hard for freedom of the press. He believed he had the right to say whatever he wished – however controversial – and he did.

Wilkes entered Parliament in 1757 as MP for Aylesbury, his home town at the time.

He started making enemies following the launch of *The North Briton* in 1762, a political weekly run with the help of friend Charles Churchill, who, like Wilkes, was a member of the infamous Hell-Fire Club at Medmenham Abbey and later West Wycombe.

The newspaper was produced in response to *The Briton*, a weekly periodical set up in the interests of political opponent, the Earl of Bute, and edited by novelist Tobias Smollett. In comparison to Smollett's dull publication, *The North Briton* was full of wit and became a major hit. It contained ferocious attacks on Bute's failing government and the people could not get enough of it.

However, the forty-fifth issue was deemed to have overstepped the mark. It was claimed to be seditious and libellous against Bute's government and the king himself. Wilkes was arrested and imprisoned in the Tower. Though the writer was soon released – his arrest was judged to be illegal – he was eventually expelled from the House in 1764 following the publication of *Essay on Woman*, a parody of Alexander Pope's *Essay on Man*. The MP's opponents believed that Wilkes had again gone too far and labelled the work 'an obscene libel'.

Wilkes spent much of his latter life on the Continent, but he did return to politics as an MP for Middlesex and remained as popular as ever among the common man. The prolific pamphleteer always wrote to and for the people, relentlessly attacking his political opponents, and he was rarely out of trouble because of his pen.

Prebendal House, where John Wilkes resided.

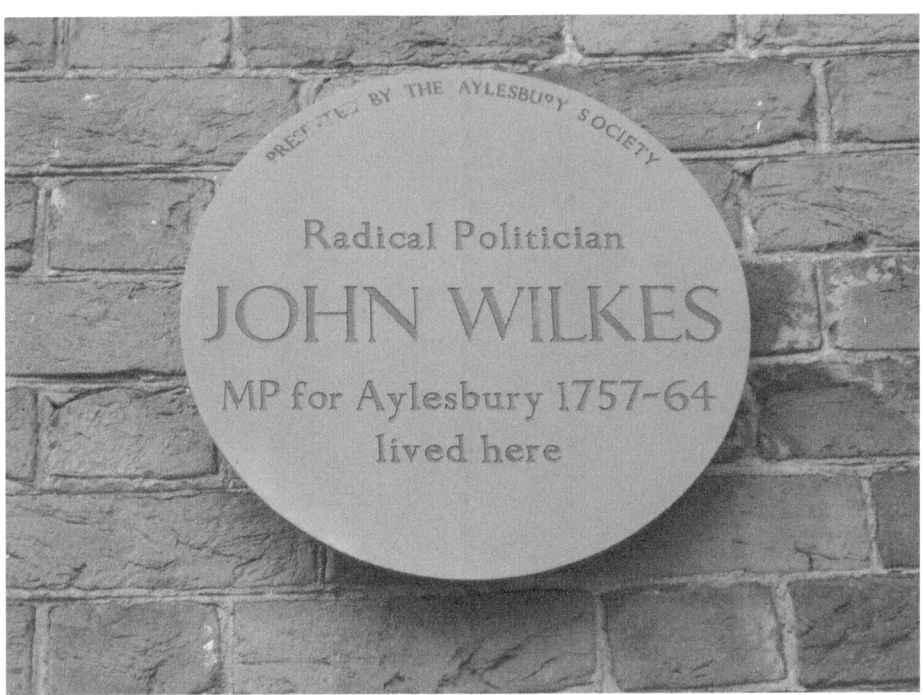

Wilkes also served Aylesbury as a magistrate and was held within high regard throughout the town. Prebendal House – where he lived – is situated close to St Mary's Church. Wilkes died in London and is buried in the capital.

Poet Winthrop Mackworth Praed was MP for Aylesbury from 1837 until his untimely death two years later. Praed, who founded the periodical *Etonian*, is remembered for his humorous poems and other light verses.

Dramatist John Lyly and travel writer Austen Henry Layard also served as MPs at different periods of history.

The market town of Aylesbury honours one of the county's most famous former residents. A statue of Benjamin Disraeli, man of letters and twice prime minister, stands in the town square. Disraeli lived most of his life at Hughenden Manor, near High Wycombe.

Another famous Buckinghamshire writer is honoured at the county museum, where there is a permanent attraction for visitors. Roald Dahl lived a large part of his life at Great Missenden.

Benjamin Disraeli's statue stands proudly in the town centre.

3

Gateway to the Chilterns

The Chiltern Hills rise like mountains in contrast to the flat pastures of the Vale of Aylesbury. Though the Chilterns stretch north into Bedfordshire, many consider Ivinghoe Beacon – the starting point of two famous long-distance footpaths – to be the gateway into one of the most beautiful regions of England. Few areas have been blessed with so many literary associations. 'Welcome', as one writer declared, to the 'Country of the Larks'.

IVINGHOE

Walter Scott

It is not difficult to guess the novel that Walter Scott is supposed to have named after the village of Ivinghoe.

Reputedly, the village itself or Ivinghoe Beacon, the site of an Iron Age hill fort and one of the most visited spots in the Chiltern Hills, became the inspiration for *Ivanhoe*.

It is said that the author used the name for his title character after hearing an old rhyme about another chivalrous gentleman. There are many versions, but all declare that 'for striking the Black Prince a blow' a certain 'Hampden of Hampden did forego . . . the manors of Tring, Wing and Ivinghoe'.

The rhyme, still much quoted in these parts, is supposed to refer to an ancestor of Puritan hero John Hampden. It appears the nobleman was dispossessed of his manor for striking the Black Prince during a feat of chivalry, though the origin of the rhyme is not clear and these three villages were never, in fact, in the Hampden estate. Scott may have deliberately slightly changed the name of the village to create his most famous character or may have incorrectly remembered it.

Ivinghoe Beacon is a prominent landmark in the Chilterns and offers superb views. It is also the starting point of the Ridgeway and Icknield Way long-distance footpaths.

Ivinghoe Beacon gave its name to a Scott novel.

DRAYTON BEAUCHAMP

Richard Hooker

Richard Hooker – the greatest of the Elizabethan Anglican theologians – served the pretty Church of St Mary the Virgin in Drayton Beauchamp for a short period.

Hooker, who gained fame for his efforts in trying to bring calm during the religious turmoil following the Reformation, came here as the rector in 1584. It was his first incumbency following his studies at Oxford. He left the following year to take over as Master of the Temple Church in London.

Hooker's most famous work is *Of the Laws of Ecclesiastical Polity*, which helped steer the new Church of England between the extremes of Roman Catholicism and Puritanism.

ASTON CLINTON

Evelyn Waugh

It might not have been such a bad thing that novelist Evelyn Waugh was sacked from his teaching post at a school in Aston Clinton – after making a drunken pass at a matron – because, later that month, he wrote in his diary: 'The time has arrived to set about being a man of letters.'

Perhaps the incident, and a further spell at a state school in London, which proved to be even briefer, finally persuaded him to turn to his pen for a living. Waugh was already writing, but he had not made a name for himself at that stage. It did not take

Richard Hooker was the rector of Drayton Beauchamp.

him long to make his mark, however. *Decline and Fall*, now one of his most famous works, was published in 1928, the year after his dismissal from Aston Clinton.

Waugh became a teacher after leaving Oxford University, following many of his contemporaries into the profession. He first taught at a school in Wales before moving to Aston Clinton in September 1925. His friend, Richard Greene, who was a music teacher at the Buckinghamshire school, helped secure him the job before moving on himself. Waugh taught English, history and art for a salary of £160 per annum.

The author's experiences at Aston Clinton certainly inspired much of *Decline and Fall* and he penned some of it here, but his previous school in Wales, it appears, had the bigger influence on the work.

Waugh completed *PRB: An Essay on the Pre-Raphaelite Brotherhood* while still teaching at Aston Clinton. It is believed it took him less than a week to write, in between correcting exam papers, though he had perceived the idea for the work long before. The pamphlet eventually led to his first book, the biography *Rossetti*, which was published in 1928.

The author was a popular master at Aston Clinton and won the admiration of his pupils, their adoration fuelled by the fact he rode around the Buckinghamshire countryside on a motorcycle named 'Queensberry', which Greene left for him.

Waugh enjoyed teaching, and it must have come as a blow when he was dismissed in February 1927. Fortunately, even greater things were just around the corner and he went on to write the famous *Brideshead Revisited*.

The school was based at Aston Clinton House, a large mansion that was previously home to the Rothschild family. It was demolished in the 1950s. Green Park Training & Conference Centre now stands in its place.

Matthew Arnold

Victorian poet Matthew Arnold was a frequent visitor to the former home of the Rothschild family. Arnold was a friend of Louisa de Rothschild. The scribe met her in his role as an inspector of schools, Louisa having established a number of Jewish schools in the East End of London.

William Makepeace Thackeray

Novelist William Thackeray was another to visit Louisa de Rothschild at Aston Clinton and immortalised her in *The History of Pendennis*.

He wrote: 'I saw a Jewish lady, only yesterday, with a child at her knee, and from whose face towards the child there shone a sweetness so angelical, that it seemed to form a sort of glory round both.'

Fellow scribes Robert Browning, Thomas Babington Macaulay, Alfred Lord Tennyson and Samuel Rogers were among the other literary guests at Aston Clinton.

WENDOVER

Robert Louis Stevenson

Robert Louis Stevenson was not exactly complimentary towards Wendover. For a man of words, he did not have much to say about the town when he came in 1875, even though it is now one of the most visited in the Chilterns. He called it 'a straggling, purposeless sort of place'.

To be fair to the writer, he was actually referring to the layout of the town, rather than questioning its existence. He claimed the locals all had an 'opinion as to how the street should go'. And he was far more forthcoming of his praise when it came to the local hostelry. He stayed at the Red Lion in High Street and remarked on its comfortable parlour where he spent the evening under the spell of the landlord's little daughter, who delighted in showing him her dolls. Stevenson wrote: 'I never saw any room much more to be admired than the low wainscoted parlour in which I spent the remainder of the evening.'

The author stayed in Wendover for the night while on a walking tour of the Chilterns, which began in High Wycombe and finished in Tring, where he jumped back on the train to London. *An Autumn Effect* was the work that resulted from his rambles. It can be found in *Essays of Travel*. Stevenson called the region 'the Country of the Larks' and was far more complimentary towards the surrounding countryside.

Poet Edward Thomas also enjoyed a walking tour of the Chilterns in 1913 and wrote *The Icknield Way*, a work based on his experiences.

It seems writers have been divided in their thoughts towards Wendover over the years. Daniel Defoe called it 'a mean, dirty, corporate town', while John Leland, another who toured England with his pen, earlier described it as 'a pretty through-fayre town'. However, Richard Steele, the founder of *Tatler* and the author of *The Christian Hero*, Edmund Burke and George Canning all thought enough of Wendover to represent the town in Parliament as an MP.

Novelist P.H. Newby certainly approved of one of the residents at the very least. He married a Wendover girl at the end of the Second World War and lived in the

Robert Louis Stevenson stayed at the Red Lion.

town for a spell. Newby was the first winner of the Booker Prize in 1969 for his novel *Something to Answer For*.

Rupert Brooke

Poet Rupert Brooke, who knew the area well, was another literary guest at the Red Lion in Wendover. Brooke wrote of 'the Roman road to Wendover, by Tring and Lilley Hoo' in his 1913 poem *The Chilterns*. However, he is better associated with another Chiltern inn – the Pink & Lily at Lacey Green.

It is thought Oliver Cromwell was also once a guest of the sixteenth-century Red Lion.

Roger of Wendover

The most notable literary son of Wendover was a man known to us simply as Roger. Roger of Wendover was one of the first historians in literature. His best-known work is *Flowers of History*, a chronicle of the history of England. Much of what we know about King John is down to Roger, who is thought to have lived in the first half of the thirteenth century. Though nothing is known about his early life in Wendover, Roger went on to become a monk at St Albans and was also historiographer to Henry III at one point.

ELLESBOROUGH

Thomas Edwards

The parish church at Ellesborough is the resting place of eighteenth-century poet Thomas Edwards. Edwards, who lived the latter part of his life at a small farm in the vicinity, devoted his retirement to writing sonnets, one of the few men of his time to preserve this form of poetry.

CHEQUERS

Winston Churchill

Chequers has been the official country residence for British prime ministers since David Lloyd George first came here in 1921. Many who followed considered themselves skilled with the pen and few have not been tempted to write their memoirs at the very least! Winston Churchill was perhaps the most successful twentieth-century prime minister to pick up a pen. He wrote history books and biographies.

Chequers can be viewed from the road, but the best vantage point is from the heights of Coombe Hill, which is topped by its famous war memorial, a visible landmark for many miles around. Coombe Hill is the highest point in the Chilterns.

GREAT KIMBLE

William Shakespeare

It is said that the castle of King Cunobelinus or Cymbeline, ruler of much of southern Britain, once stood on a hill above Great Kimble. Little Kimble and Great Kimble are said to have derived their names from the king, whose life forms the basis of the well-known Shakespeare play, *Cymbeline*.

Cymbeline's Mount, the only visible evidence a castle may have stood here, sits at the shoulder of Beacon Hill, its larger neighbouring mound, from which there are superb views. A public footpath close to Ellesborough Church – the place of worship for prime ministers in residence at nearby Chequers – takes the walker between Cymbeline's Mount and towering Beacon Hill.

ASTON SANDFORD

Thomas Scott

The tiny Church of St Michael & All Angels in Aston Sandford is the final resting place of 'the Commentator'. The Revd Thomas Scott was the author of *Commentary on the Bible*, which first appeared in weekly parts from 1788 and was later published in six volumes. The work was once heralded as 'the greatest theological performance of the age and country'.

Scott was already a well-known writer and celebrated Evangelical scholar when he came to quiet Aston Sandford. He had earlier served the Buckinghamshire parishes

Cymbeline's Mount, once fit for a king.

of Stoke Goldington, Weston Underwood and Ravenstone, before succeeding hymn-writer John Newton as the curate at Olney.

Scott eventually moved to London where he wrote his famous *Commentary*. He came to Aston Sandford in 1801 and died there some twenty years later. His grandson, George Gilbert Scott, the famous architect and a writer himself, described his grandfather as 'a thin tottering old man, very grave and dignified'.

The rector's funeral had to be held at Haddenham, as his church at Aston Sandford was too small to accommodate the large crowds who wished to pay their respects. The great Bible scholar was, however, buried inside St Michael's, where there is a memorial to him.

PRINCES RISBOROUGH

Winifred Holtby

Novelist and essayist Winifred Holtby came to the Princes Risborough area towards the end of her life. She spent her final few years bravely fighting illness and convalesced at Whiteleaf for a period in 1932. She died in a London nursing home some three years later.

Her most famous novel was her final one, *South Riding*, which was published posthumously. The work centres around a strong-willed headmistress and is set in Yorkshire, the author's native county.

This part of Buckinghamshire, and beyond the Oxfordshire border towards Chinnor, was an area much loved by children's author Elsie J. Oxenham.

She set her famous 'Abbey' books in the region, fondly describing the beechwoods and pretty villages, which she had herself visited as a child in the late nineteenth century.

GREAT HAMPDEN

Thomas Carlyle

Puritan hero John Hampden became the subject matter for many writers, including historian Thomas Carlyle.

Hampden gained fame for an act of defiance towards Charles I, which helped fuel the approaching Civil War. The Parliamentarian, who resided at Hampden House, refused to pay Ship Money, a tax to support the navy, which the king 'unlawfully' extended inland. His enemies believed it to be just another act of tyranny and Hampden refused to accept it. Judges ruled against the landowner, but the narrow court victory for the king only helped to increase Hampden's popularity and undermine England's absolute monarchy. Ultimately, it led to civil war. Hampden fought for the Parliamentarians and was fatally wounded at Chalgrove Field in 1643. He died six days later in Thame.

An account of Hampden's refusal to pay Ship Money can be found in Carlyle's *Oliver Cromwell's Letters and Speeches*. The historian claimed: 'Mr Hampden became the most famous man in England, by accident partly.'

Many writers have recorded the story of Hampden and he remains a champion of the common people. Statesman and philosopher Edmund Burke famously stated: 'Would 20 shillings have ruined Mr Hampden's fortune? No, but the payment of half 20 shillings, on the principle it was demanded, would have made him a slave.'

Hampden House – television buffs may recognise it as the headquarters and star of many of the Hammer House of Horror productions – is not open to the public, but can be viewed from a footpath close by. Hampden was buried at the

Hampden House, home of a very famous Puritan.

church opposite the house. A stone obelisk, just off the road to Prestwood, is easily missed. It is almost hidden in a small hedged enclosure, but a plaque here records: 'For these lands in Stoke Mandeville, John Hampden was assessed in 20 shillings Ship Money levied by command of the King without authority of law.' However, the Church of St Nicholas at Great Kimble claims to be the spot where Hampden publicly announced his refusal to pay Ship Money. There is also a bronze statue of perhaps Buckinghamshire's most famous son in Market Square, Aylesbury.

Richard Baxter

Puritan preacher and writer Richard Baxter stayed as a guest of Richard Hampden at Hampden House to escape the plague. Baxter knew John Hampden well and, long after the latter's death, highlighted his popularity. The author recalled Hampden as 'having the most universal praise of any gentleman that I remember of that age'.

Baxter was a prolific writer of devotional literature. His most famous work is *The Saint's Everlasting Rest*. Baxter knew the Chilterns well and preached in the area, notably at Amersham.

John Masefield

One can easily picture sailor-poet John Masefield and his family at Rectory Farm, Great Hampden. Rupert Brooke, a frequent visitor, wrote a letter during one visit. 'I sit in front of the cottage writing . . . Mr Masefield is inside, singing sea shanties to the baby [their son Lewis].' One only hopes that particular shanty was a little tamer than Masefield's famous seafaring tales that made it into print, for he was not one to mince his words.

A stone obelisk honours Hampden's defiance.

Masefield and his wife Constance shared the house with a close friend. The author described the residence in 1909 as 'a lovely little farm in Buckinghamshire, high up on a chalk hill surrounded by beechwoods and common land, a very fresh, pretty, but rather bare and cold country like most chalk hills'. The Masefields moved to Great Hampden in that year and the property remained a holiday home until about 1913, by which time they were enjoying more prosperity.

At the time of their arrival, Masefield was struggling to support the family with his pen. He had published nothing of note since *Salt-Water Ballads* some seven years earlier. He had almost come to the conclusion that his gift had deserted him, but the peaceful surroundings of the Chilterns helped to fire his imagination. It was here that Masefield reputedly gained the inspiration for *The Everlasting Mercy*, his most famous narrative poem. The work, published in 1911, marked the turning point in his career and he never looked back.

Much of Masefield's poetry reflected his love for the countryside. It is thought that part of *Reynard the Fox* was written at Great Hampden. Though the places in the poem are fictitious, Masefield may have been thinking of Long Crendon and the Aylesbury Vale when penning the famous opening line of part two: 'On old Cold Crendon's windy tops.'

LACEY GREEN

Rupert Brooke

Few loved the Chiltern Hills as much as poet Rupert Brooke, and few loved the Pink & Lily pub as much either. Brooke liked nothing more than roaming the beautiful countryside and then rewarding himself with a drink...or two...or three...

The Pink & Lily is situated at Parslow's Hillock, high in the hills above Princess Risborough, on the Lacey Green to Great Hampden road. Brooke used to travel from his Grantchester home to Wendover and make the journey to the pub on foot, taking in the wonderful scenery on the way.

It is not known how the poet discovered the Pink & Lily. He may have just come upon it during one of his many rambles, or fellow writer John Masefield, who lived nearby at Great Hampden, may have introduced him to it. But once he found it, Brooke thought nothing of incorporating it into his frequent treks from Wendover, and he would spend hours between opening times walking in the surrounding countryside.

The Pink & Lily, in Pink Road, became the subject of a couple of light-hearted verses from Brooke's pen. Most famous are the simple words he wrote with French painter and drinking companion Jacques Raverat:

> Never came there to the Pink
> Two men such as we, I think
> Never came there to the Lily
> Two men quite so richly silly.

It was not Brooke's most enduring verse and was no doubt written after indulging in one drink too many. His poem *The Chilterns*, dated 1913, is perhaps a little more

Poet Rupert Brooke came to the Pink & Lily, as the inn sign recalls.

worthy of mention. Brooke wrote: 'I shall desire and I shall find . . . The best of my desires.' Those desires included 'laughter and inn-fires', and many would agree that there is nothing better than ending a country walk in a cosy Chiltern pub.

Brooke also spent much time in the area with sweetheart Cathleen Nesbitt. She wrote: 'We felt our souls communing in the air.' These were happy days for Brooke, but the First World War was to put an end to them and, tragically, to the poet too.

Fellow poet Matthew Arnold is believed to have been another regular visitor to the Pink & Lily.

SPEEN

Samuel Pepys

The Pink & Lily is not the only hostelry in the area to have delighted a man of letters.

The Old Plow, which dates from the seventeenth century, is situated in the hamlet of Flowers Bottom below Speen. Samuel Pepys is said to have written part of his diary sitting next to the enormous bread oven.

Anna Sewell

The Home of Rest for Horses at Speen is not the most obvious place to find a literary connection. The home was founded in 1886 by Ann Lindo and had a number of bases in the capital before locating here.

Ann shared a love of horses and a concern for their humane treatment with well-known Quaker Anna Sewell, author of *Black Beauty*, which was published in 1877 just before her death. Some have suggested that the two women may have met because of their common cause. No doubt, at the very least, Ann would have known all about the novel and may have been partly inspired by it to do something positive.

Black Beauty was originally written for the benefit of those who worked with horses. The author herself wrote that the aim of the novel was 'to induce kindness, sympathy, and an understanding treatment of horses'. The Home of Rest for Horses is open to the public.

Samuel Pepys wrote part of his diary at the Old Plow.

Eric Gill

Controversial sculptor and typographer Eric Gill, who also made his name with his pen, moved to Upper North Dean in 1928. He lived at Pigotts – situated up a steep lane off the road to Speen – until his death in 1940.

Gill set up a printing press and wrote a number of essays here. The collection of brick buildings set around a farmhouse served as workshops for his little band of stonemasons. Gill was buried at Speen Baptist Church. His grave is situated at the far end of the churchyard.

GREAT MISSENDEN

Roald Dahl

You can hardly accuse Roald Dahl of just pottering about when he went to the garden shed. While many of the male of the species merely seek sanctuary within the walls of this great British institution, the creative Dahl set about establishing himself as one of the country's most popular writers when he came to his particular refuge each morning.

His writing hut, which he himself adapted from a garden shed after moving to Little Whitefield in the mid-1950s, still stands. In it, Dahl, with his pencils neatly arranged beside him, wrote endearing children's classics such as *Charlie and the Chocolate Factory* and *The BFG*.

Eric Gill is buried at Speen.

Dahl, the son of Norwegian parents, lived in Great Missenden until his death in 1990. He said of his unusual working place: 'It's marvellous, isolated, quiet.' All that disturbed him was the occasional heifer from the adjacent orchard. He said he could sometimes hear their tongues scraping against the window and they would eat the curtains if he left it open. As a child, Dahl used to hide up a tree in order to write his diary and, as an adult, it is clear that he continued to find inspiration while shutting the world out.

The author's home in Whitefield Lane was once known as Gipsy House and Dahl adopted the old name in 1963. The garden contained an old gipsy caravan when he moved in and many will immediately think of the libertarian father of *Danny, the Champion of the World* who creeps out of his own gipsy caravan at night to go poaching in the woods. The book perhaps best highlights the author's love of the Chilterns, as it contains many references to Great Missenden and the surrounding area.

Dahl also wrote much for adults and became extremely wealthy when he penned the screenplay for the James Bond film, *You Only Live Twice*, even though he said he found the idea 'exceptionally distasteful'. A chauffeur-driven Rolls-Royce would arrive in Great Missenden to pick the author up when he was working on the script. Dahl is also said to have disliked the film version of *Charlie and the Chocolate Factory* when it appeared in 1971, but it too increased his worldwide fame.

The author continued to write until his final days, penning numerous stories for children, which appear to grow in popularity over the years. He is buried at St Peter & St Paul's Church on the hill above the town. Great Missenden now honours its famous former resident in The Roald Dahl Museum and Story Centre, which is situated in High Street. Visitors will have little trouble locating it, as some of the author's characters create a brash exterior wall. Among the attractions is a replica of Dahl's famous writing hut.

Robert Louis Stevenson

Robert Louis Stevenson stayed in Great Missenden while on his walking tour of the Chilterns in 1875. In *An Autumn Effect* – the essay that resulted from his trip – he informs us that he arrived during the afternoon. The fair was in town and he remarked on a number of stalls selling pastries and other goods. Stevenson wrote: 'The sleepy hum of a threshing-machine filled the neighbouring fields and hung about the quaint street corners.'

The author also ventured out after dark and admits to peeping through a window where he watches a woman reading a story to a child. The landlady at the inn where he stayed complained about her cabbages being ruined by caterpillars.

Antiquary John Leland described Great Missenden as 'a quiet old-fashioned place, with no actual picturesque features, but reposeful with its unostentatious dwellings grouped below the beechwoods'.

Above: *Gipsy House, the home of Roald Dahl.*

Right: *Dahl is buried in Great Missenden parish churchyard.*

A museum is now devoted to Roald Dahl in Great Missenden.

HOLMER GREEN

Christina Rossetti

English literature will forever be indebted to Holmer Green, as the village played a huge part in the career of one of our best-loved poets.

Christina Rossetti said herself that visits as a child to see her grandfather at Holmer Green inspired her pen in later life. She wrote: 'If one thing schooled me in the direction of poetry it was perhaps the delightful liberty to prowl all alone about my grandfather's cottage grounds some 30 miles from London.'

Grandfather Gaetano Polidori, himself a writer, retired here in 1836, some six years after the birth of Christina. She only had the pleasure of these country trips – which entailed a long stagecoach journey – for a few years, as her grandfather returned to London in 1839, when Christina was just 9 years old. But Holmer Green instilled into her a love of nature and she fondly recalled happy holidays here. She wrote that the grounds were simple and quite small, 'but to me they were vast, varied and worth exploring'. There was nothing Christina and brother Dante Gabriel Rossetti enjoyed more than their visits to Holmer Green.

Sadly, the house no longer exists, but street names – such as Rossetti Place – honour the village's most famous visitor, as does the parish hall, which is also now named after the poet.

4

Heart of
the Chilterns

Busy High Wycombe is regarded as the heart of the Chilterns. It is certainly the biggest town in the region and an ideal base from which to explore. There are literary connections in every direction and in the town itself.

Hughenden became home to perhaps the Chilterns' most famous literary resident, a writer who was twice to become prime minister. Meanwhile, a less well-known scribe, more remembered for his hell-raising exploits, also thought enough of West Wycombe to leave his heart there – literally!

HIGH WYCOMBE

John Wesley

Preacher and writer John Wesley became the inspiration to many as he toured Buckinghamshire. High Wycombe became one of his favourite locations and he is said to have come here at least thirty times to preach.

Among the congregation on one occasion was Hannah Ball. It is a name not familiar to many, but she became the pioneer of a great British institution that is still thriving today – the Sunday school movement. Many claim Robert Raikes as the instigator, but it is believed Hannah started her Sunday school in High Wycombe some eleven years before Raikes's school at Gloucester.

A plaque in Queen Square, above a shop in the centre of High Wycombe, declares that Hannah lived here between 1759 and 1766. She was lodging with her widowed brother and his children at the time. It was during her spell here that she got up early one morning in order to listen to Wesley preaching in the town. Because of his hectic schedule, he was due to talk at 5 a.m. It was a morning that was to change her life forever. Hannah was to become one of the preacher's earliest converts to Methodism.

Wesley wrote that she 'had a peculiar love for children and a talent for assisting them'. Her Sunday school is believed to have started in 1769, though it may have been even earlier. She also played a big part in the planting of a Methodist chapel in

High Wycombe. Wesley preached at the opening service. The chapel, once in St Mary Street, no longer exists and the current home of the Methodists is now in Priory Road, the new church named in honour of the founder of the faith.

Hannah and Wesley became good friends and remained correspondents throughout their lives. One of Wesley's final letters to Hannah, when her health was fading, was typically encouraging and hopeful: 'Look up, my dear friend, the prize is before us, we are on the point of parting no more. In time and eternity you will be united with your ever affectionate brother, John Wesley.'

Hannah was buried at St Peter & St Paul's Church at nearby Stokenchurch, the resting place of other members of her family. Her faded gravestone is one of five in a row close to the church itself.

Not everyone in High Wycombe welcomed Wesley with open arms. The town's museum once displayed a drum that belonged to a resident hostile to non-conformists. He would order it to be beaten in the hope of drowning out the preacher's sermons.

Wesley was one of many illustrious visitors to Loakes, the splendid home of former prime minister, Lord Shelburne, who lived here between 1761 and 1798 according to a plaque adorning the entrance to what is now Wycombe Abbey School. Wesley admired the grounds and declared: 'What variety in so small a compass!'

Other literary guests to Loakes included Samuel Johnson, James Boswell, Edmund Burke, Benjamin Franklin, Oliver Goldsmith and Joseph Priestley.

Ivor Gurney

A plaque on a modest house in The Greenway records that poet and composer Ivor Gurney lived here between 1913 and 1915. Gurney left High Wycombe to serve in the First World War, which became the inspiration for most of his poems. Sadly, the writer suffered from mental problems for much of his life, though he continued to write and compose.

Samuel Taylor Coleridge

One would not expect a Romantic poet to be best suited to a life as a soldier. And so it proved for Samuel Taylor Coleridge. He only served the Light Dragoons for a few months, when it became obvious to all that his talents lay elsewhere. Coleridge, probably because of debt, enlisted in 1793 under a false name. It is believed that he was quartered at an inn in Easton Street.

Edmund Waller

Poet Edmund Waller was a pupil at the old Royal Grammar School. The school was built incorporating the medieval Hospital of St John the Baptist before being demolished towards the end of the nineteenth century and relocated to a newer building in the grounds. Some remains of the hospital, and the new building, can be seen in Easton Street. The current grammar school is now situated at the top of Amersham Hill. Waller repaid the town for his education by later becoming its MP.

T.S. Eliot

T.S. Eliot endured a very brief spell as a teacher at the new Royal Grammar School in Amersham Hill. He came here at the start of the autumn term in 1915, but did

The High Wycombe home of Ivor Gurney.

not stay long. The poet eventually left the profession for banking. He is reputed to have said working in a bank was like a holiday compared to teaching!

Eliot was living in London at the time, but would often stay overnight in High Wycombe, renting lodgings in Conegra Road.

A number of literary figures appear in a stained-glass window in All Saints' Church, which sits in the centre of High Wycombe. The window pays tribute to the role of women in ministering to others. Emily Brontë, Christina Rossetti and Elizabeth Fry are among those that take pride of place. The window was donated by the influential Frances Dove, founder of Wycombe Abbey School and the town's first woman councillor, who herself overcame much prejudice.

William Cobbett

Be careful not to mess with the women of High Wycombe because essayist William Cobbett suggested that the fairer sex were not as petite as those found in other areas.

In *Rural Rides*, Cobbett declared: 'Wycombe is a very fine and very clean market town; the people all looking extremely well; the girls somewhat larger featured and larger boned than those in Sussex, and nor so fresh-coloured and bright-eyed.'

BRADENHAM

Benjamin Disraeli and Isaac D'Israeli

Novelist and former prime minister Benjamin Disraeli never forgot his old home at Bradenham.

T.S. Eliot taught at the Royal Grammar School.

Endymion, which was published the year before his death, highlights the affection he held for the family residence. Bradenham was disguised as Hurstley in the work and the author fondly recalled the old manor house that was once his home. Disraeli was in his mid-70s and living at nearby Hughenden Manor when he penned the novel, but the idyllic surroundings of his former abode were evidently never far from his mind.

While living at Bradenham House, Disraeli wrote to his sister during a trip to Europe on one occasion. 'There is no place like Bradenham,' the homesick brother declared.

Father Isaac D'Israeli (Benjamin dropped the apostrophe) brought the family to Bradenham in 1829. It seemed a strange move at the time. Isaac was in his mid-60s and had a large circle of friends in London. Literally overnight, he swapped his hectic social life for a solitary existence in a secluded country setting. He rarely ventured further than the garden and took little interest in outside affairs.

Isaac already knew Buckinghamshire thanks to poet Henry James Pye, who had introduced him to John Penn, of Stoke Poges, the grandson of pioneer and Quaker William Penn. The family spent a short spell at Hyde Heath, near Chesham, before finding the home of their dreams.

Isaac became blind in his latter years, but was content. His passion was literary history and he wrote much on the subject before his death (at Bradenham House in 1848), his most famous work being *Curiosities of Literature*. There is a huge monument to him on a hill above Downley that overlooks Hughenden Manor. It is further evidence he was a man of letters in his own right and not just the father of one who was to gain even more success. The monument was actually erected by Benjamin's wife, Mary Anne, and honours Isaac, 'who, by his happy genius, diffused among the multitude that elevating taste for literature which before his time was the privilege only of the learned'.

Bradenham House was much loved by Benjamin Disraeli.

A monument honours Isaac D'Israeli.

There is no doubt that Benjamin was one of those inspired by his father. He inherited his love of books and respect for nature, in particular, trees. His own love for the Chilterns, an affair which lasted a lifetime, grew from his many rambles on the hills and surrounding beechwoods. Unlike his father, he did not become a recluse. The publication of *Vivian Grey* in 1826 had already helped to make his name in the capital. Bradenham simply became a temporary escape, a place where he could mull over ideas for his novels and his political aspirations. One can easily picture the ambitious Disraeli strolling over the hills, dreaming of grandeur.

The young author-politician initially had more joy in his literary career than his political one. He made several unsuccessful attempts to become the MP for High Wycombe before being given the chance to represent Maidstone in 1837. His political ideas appeared in most of his novels. *Coningsby*, *Sybil* and *Tancred* were all published before he left Bradenham for nearby Hughenden Manor.

HUGHENDEN MANOR

Benjamin Disraeli

There is no doubt that Hughenden Manor is a home fit for a prime minister, and Benjamin Disraeli believed he was fit to inhabit it.

Though not wealthy when he came here with his family in 1848, shortly after the publication of *Tancred*, he was of the opinion that a leading Conservative politician – he was not yet prime minister – should have a stately home to show off. Disraeli, always aware of his Jewish descent, longed to be an English gentleman and he was to spend the remaining thirty-three years of his life here.

The author never lost his passion for the Chilterns, and trees in particular. He planted many in the grounds of Hughenden Manor, often to commemorate visits from friends. 'I have a passion for books and trees,' he wrote. After he had returned from a long spell at Westminster, he would spend 'the first week back examining his trees, and the second week examining his books'.

Disraeli particularly loved the gardens and said: 'We have made a garden of terraces, in which cavaliers might roam and saunter, with their lady-loves.' Peacocks also strutted their stuff here. 'You cannot have a terrace without peacocks,' he insisted.

The house itself underwent a radical transformation to suit the taste of this rather pompous dandy. It became a showy and, some would say, unattractive Gothic mansion.

Disraeli was twice prime minister, in 1868 and from 1874–80. From 1876, he took the title Earl of Beaconsfield when he entered the House of Lords, rather than Lord Bradenham or Lord Hughenden.

Not surprisingly, a number of important visitors came to Hughenden. Queen Victoria would have taken tea in the drawing room and also came a few days after Disraeli's funeral. The author was buried at St Michael & All Angels' Church, which sits on the hillside below the house. The family tomb can be seen outside, under the chapel window. The vault was opened in order that Queen Victoria could lay some china flowers upon the coffin of her great friend. In the church itself, she also placed a memorial above the seat Disraeli occupied.

Above: *Hughenden Manor, home
of Benjamin Disraeli.*

Right: *Disraeli is buried at
Hughenden's pretty church.*

Disraeli left instructions to be buried quietly, so there was no state funeral, but, fittingly for this charismatic man of letters, it was still an impressive affair. Members of the royal family and ambassadors from around the world were in attendance.

Hughenden Manor and its vast grounds are today in the care of the National Trust. The house, unlike the one at Bradenham, is open to the public, with visitors flocking to pay homage to one of the most famous of all Chiltern residents.

WEST WYCOMBE

Hell-Fire Club

To say poet and pamphleteer Paul Whitehead put his heart into the infamous Hell-Fire Club would perhaps be an understatement. He literally gave his heart to it!

The Hell-Fire Club was founded by Francis Dashwood, the owner of West Wycombe House. Its motto was 'Do What Thou Wilt' and members appear to have done just that. Excessive drinking and wild orgies were credited among their activities. A number of eminent people, including politicians and statesmen, held membership. Whitehead was among the many writers who indulged in its pleasures.

Sir Francis built the Dashwood Mausoleum, which stands beside the Church of St Lawrence on a crest overlooking West Wycombe, in 1765. The urns in the alcoves were going to hold the hearts of each member following their deaths, but all are empty now. It is thought that Whitehead was the only one to have his heart removed and placed in one of the urns following his demise. The rather gruesome artefact lured many tourists in the nineteenth century. The heart was frequently taken out of the urn to satisfy the curiosity of the sightseers. Over the years it must have shrivelled up considerably, for it was reported that one visitor described it as being the size of a walnut. It still must have held some fascination to someone, however, as the heart is believed to have been stolen at some point.

Whitehead was one of the principal members of the Hell-Fire Club and perhaps its most enthusiastic supporter. He was responsible for organising activities and drawing up a code of conduct. The writer was also the most loyal friend of Dashwood and dedicated *The Poems and Miscellaneous Compositions of Paul Whitehead* to the leader of the club.

Dashwood never had a bad word to say against Whitehead and provided him with a home at West Wycombe House in his latter years. When the poet died in 1774, a lavish service, full of pomp and ceremony, was held at St Lawrence Church, much to the disgust of the villagers. They resented the 'evil influence' Whitehead had had on their squire and one remarked that if they could see the heart that was to be placed in the mausoleum, 'it would appear as black in death as it had been in life'.

Francis Dashwood, who was born in 1708, was a writer himself. In his youth, he penned republican and anti-court sentiments in verse. Like many of the members of the Hell-Fire Club, he enjoyed a life in politics, becoming an MP and then Chancellor of the Exchequer in 1762.

The activities of the Hell-Fire Club outraged many, but it is difficult to ascertain where truth ends and legend begins. The club met in secret and, though there is little

The Dashwood Mausoleum at West Wycombe.

doubt the goings-on during meetings would not have appealed to most, local gossip may have exaggerated the truth.

Dashwood had a reputation for opposing organised religion. He was certainly an anti-Papist and there is evidence to suggest that black magic was one activity carried out by members of the club. However, he may have been merely a liberal reformer when it came to church affairs and not the Satanist many have labelled him. In 1773, he worked with close friend Benjamin Franklin on penning a simplified version of the *Book of Common Prayer*, which is still in use throughout America. The aim, as he himself put it, was to prevent the 'old and faithful' from freezing to death in cold churches by making services shorter, which would also attract the 'young and lively' and 'retrieve the well-disposed from the infliction of interminable prayer'. Dashwood was already working on the book before Franklin came to assist, though the latter is usually given more of the credit for it these days.

Visitors to West Wycombe can see the influence of Dashwood all around. West Wycombe House, now in the care of the National Trust and open to the public, is set in magnificent landscaped gardens complete with statues, grottoes and an ornamental lake. It is still home to the Dashwood family.

A path on the other side of the road leads up to the Dashwood Mausoleum – where Sir Francis was laid to rest – and St Lawrence Church. The church is a striking landmark, largely due to the golden ball that sits on top of its tower. Dashwood virtually rebuilt the church and added this strange feature, which is big enough to hold several people. Members of the Hell-Fire Club met in it and drank away the hours.

The revolutionary design of the church is typical of Dashwood and appears to be a deliberate statement against conformism. The poet Charles Churchill, another literary member of the club, described it as: 'A temple built aloft in air . . . That serves for show and not for prayer.'

*The Hell-Fire Club's most
novel meeting place.*

Churchill was a close associate of John Wilkes, the radical politician and pamphleteer, and another member of the club. Both actually penned many tracts and verses lampooning the private life of Dashwood.

Underneath the church and mausoleum was the club's most famous meeting place. West Wycombe Caves, now known as the Hell-Fire Caves, are open to the public. Visitors can let their imaginations run riot, helped by life-size models of the organisation's members. Dashwood excavated the caves in the mid-1750s. Churchill refers to them in his poem *The Duellist*. This rake and rebel was an ex-clergyman who was forced into the Church by his father and soon left it when the latter died.

Another literary member was poet and dramatist Robert Lloyd. He was devastated by the death of Churchill and declared: 'From now on I have nothing to live for. I shall follow poor Charles.' And he did. He took to his bed and died very soon after. Both were only in their early 30s, but many days of dissipation had taken their toll. Lloyd wrote the comic opera *The Capricious Lovers*.

Other writers have also been linked with the club, including John Hall Stevenson, author of *Crazy Tales*, who went on to set up his own hell-fire club. Laurence Sterne, a friend of Stevenson, has also been suggested as a possible reveller, but it is unlikely either were ever actually members. Horace Walpole wrote much on the organisation and may have taken part in some of the activities, while even Franklin, the great American statesman and man of letters, could not escape suspicion over membership because of his many visits to West Wycombe House.

The Hell-Fire Club lasted for at least twenty years, but no one really knows the exact length of its existence. Certainly, the death of Dashwood himself in 1781 was the final nail in its coffin, though many members had already passed away.

*The Hell-Fire Caves, a
popular tourist attraction.*

Hell-fire clubs continued to form throughout the country, however, fuelled by gossip about the most notorious of them all. Lord Byron was among the many embroiderers of the organisation's tales and, no doubt, would have been the archetypal member if he had been alive during its existence.

IBSTONE

Rebecca West

'I write sitting in a room, 45 miles from London, which is furnished with magnificent yellow taffeta curtains trimmed with bottle-green ruching, the kitchen chair which supports me, an electric fire, and nothing else.'

Rebecca West penned those words in one of her first pieces for *The New Yorker*. She was describing Ibstone House, having just moved here following the outbreak of the Second World War. The surveyors' report on the property did not dissuade her and her husband Henry from buying a country home in the Chiltern Hills. The report noted that the fences and farm buildings were in a poor condition; there was rising damp in the house and the roof needed attention.

But Ibstone House, with its 70 acres, went on to see better days. The property, on the edge of the village, became one of the most written about and photographed homes in the years to follow, appearing in numerous publications of the day. The magazine *Housewife* described it as 'a house for the happy marriage of two people who love a home and have discovered the immortal roots of country living'.

Rebecca and Henry gave grand parties and entertained famous guests. Margaret Hodges, Rebecca's live-in secretary, said that the author's 'best times' were spent at Ibstone.

The writer certainly adapted well to country life and did her bit for the community. She instigated a branch of the Women's Institute in the village and became its chairman. She even wrote a play – *Our Village* – for the WI Drama Festival, herself and Margaret taking roles in it.

Rebecca loved walking her dog in the surrounding fields and woods, though it was her cat that gained literary fame. Pounce was immortalised in Rebecca's *Letter from England* column in *The New Yorker*. The feline-loving author Paul Gallico addressed his thank-you letters to Pounce following his visits to Ibstone House.

Rebecca sold Ibstone House shortly after the death of Henry in 1968 and moved to London.

Perhaps unfairly, the author's reputation today partly rests on her earlier relationship with H.G. Wells than for the many novels and essays she went on to write.

TURVILLE

Philip Sidney and Percy Bysshe Shelley

Two famous poets from different eras have links with the pretty village of Turville and one of its most influential former residents. William Perry, who built Turville Park and settled here in the eighteenth century, married a descendant of Elizabethan poet, Philip Sidney. Their daughter then married the grandfather of Percy Bysshe Shelley.

Turville Park, situated at Turville Heath, is not open to the public, but visitors flock to the village of Turville itself. They are rarely checking out the many Sidney connections at charming St Mary's Church, however. Though descendants of the popular courtier and scribe – who fought for Queen Elizabeth and was killed in action abroad – worshipped here, most come to see the church itself due to its starring role in the television comedy, *The Vicar of Dibley*.

The nearby windmill also draws admiring sightseers, who recognise it from the 1968 film *Chitty Chitty Bang Bang*.

Poet Percy Bysshe Shelley is linked with lovely Turville.

5

Metroland

Chesham and Amersham are terminals on the Metropolitan Line of the London Underground.

In the first half of the twentieth century, the Metropolitan Railway, which once extended further into Buckinghamshire, produced books to encourage people to take the train out of London and explore the Chiltern countryside. Metroland was the name given to the area north-west of the capital. It also incorporated parts of Middlesex and Hertfordshire. Many took up the invitation and some even set up home here.

Poet John Betjeman, who immortalised the area in a television series, famously wrote in *Summoned by Bells*: 'Metroland beckoned us out to lanes in beechy Bucks.'

This corner of Buckinghamshire is also known for its religious dissention, a subject that could not fail to inspire many words.

CHESHAM

Lewis Carroll

It is not known whether Lewis Carroll ever visited Chesham, but he certainly knew all about its most famous resident of the seventeenth century.

Roger Crabbe was a hatter by trade, who suffered severe head injuries while serving the Parliamentarians during the Civil War. Oliver Cromwell sentenced him to death for a breach of discipline, but the sentence was commuted to two years' imprisonment. On his release, Crabbe's Chesham business thrived and he became one of the wealthiest tradesmen in the town.

Unfortunately, the bang on the head he received is thought to have brought on a number of eccentricities in his character. He wore sackcloth and lived on a diet of roots, herbs and grass.

Mad he may have been, but Crabbe, who later retired to Ickenham, Middlesex, for a life as a hermit, was also a generous man. He declared that he could live on three farthings a day and is believed to have given the rest of his income to the poor. Despite his generosity, his eccentricity aroused suspicion and he suffered much persecution.

The literary connection (in case you are still wondering), is that Roger Crabbe is reputed to have been the inspiration for a certain mad hatter in Lewis Carroll's *Alice in Wonderland*.

John Foxe

The death of Thomas Harding, perhaps Chesham's most famous resident, was recorded in one of the most gruesome books ever penned.

John Foxe was responsible for *Foxe's Book of Martyrs*, later published as *Acts and Monuments*. The work, which proved incredibly popular in Puritan households when it was published during the sixteenth century and long after the author's death, stoked up much anti-Catholic sentiment with its graphic descriptions of heroic Protestant martyrdom. No gory detail was omitted and Foxe pulled no punches.

Harding was a Lollard, a follower of the teachings of the great reformer and Bible translator John Wycliffe. He was discovered in the vicinity of Hodds Wood to the south of the town reading an English religious book – an act considered to be heresy – and was taken back to his house where, according to Foxe, 'certain English books of Holy Scripture' were discovered under the floorboards.

The memorial to martyr Thomas Harding.

As well as works from the pen of Wycliffe, Harding also owned tracts written by fellow reformer William Tyndale. Foxe claimed that Harding was reading Tyndale's controversial *Obedience of a Christian Man* when he was arrested.

The translation of Scripture into English, or even being in possession of such 'heresy', was still illegal and Harding was taken away for questioning before eventually being sentenced to death. It is believed that he spent his final night imprisoned in St Mary's Church, which still dominates the old part of town. Though already an old man, the authorities showed no mercy and he was burned at the stake at White Hill on the road to Botley in 1532. A memorial stone opposite the White Hill Centre now marks the spot.

Harding, who is believed to have farmed land at Dungrove, became an inspiration to many Chesham dissenters in the years to follow. It is thought that he was buried in St Mary's churchyard, where an Ionic cross was erected in the twentieth century as a tribute. A local school is also now named in his honour.

Neighbouring Amersham was a particular stronghold for Lollardy and even more suffered for their beliefs there.

William Cobbett was impressed with his visit to Chesham. He wrote that it was 'a nice little town, lying in a deep and narrow valley, with a stream of water running through it'.

D.H. Lawrence

Walk the country lanes on the outskirts of Chesham in early autumn and you will see an abundance of blackberries. But few residents were picking them in 1914.

The arrival of D.H. Lawrence and his German wife Frieda to the area aroused much suspicion and prejudice. War had just broken out and locals were less than enamoured that one of the 'enemy' was in their midst. Ridiculous gossip and tales were fabricated, the biggest concoction being that the Lawrences were poisoning the berries in the hedges. The poor newcomers became the victims of much anti-German propaganda and Lawrence wrote: 'We are so miserable about the war.'

The couple's stay in the area was a brief one. They came in late summer and were gone by January the following year. They were looking for somewhere cheap outside London where Lawrence could write and where the couple could lie low until the end of the war. Like most at the time, they had no idea the hostilities would go on for as long as they did.

The farm cottage the Lawrences rented was called The Triangle. There is no property of that name today. It is believed to have stood close to Chesham on the road to Bellingdon, and become a victim of development. However, there is also a claim that it is one of the few cottages still standing in what is now Hawridge Lane in Bellingdon itself.

The property is said to have belonged to a friend of Gilbert Cannan, the novelist who lived at nearby Cholesbury. John Middleton Murry and Katherine Mansfield also lived in the area on at least two occasions. Frieda recalled one of their few happy experiences here, when they walked through wet fields in the gloomy twilight to visit their dear friends.

Of the Lawrences' new abode, it was a 'tiny, but jolly' residence according to the author. However, novelist Compton Mackenzie, one of the first visitors, declared it to

D.H. Lawrence is reputed to have lived in Hawridge Lane.

be the ugliest cottage he had ever seen and Lawrence was himself soon calling it 'this God-forsaken little hole'.

The property, which stood in an overgrown and decaying orchard, was cramped and damp, and, by the end of January, the couple had left for a cottage in Sussex. Lawrence, whose health had been poor here, declared: 'My dear God, I've been miserable this autumn.'

The war had a big effect on the novelist and he wrote much on the subject. His experiences and reactions to it can be found in the novel *Kangaroo*, in particular. It is thought that Lawrence was working on *The Rainbow* while living at The Triangle.

CHOLESBURY

Katherine Mansfield and John Middleton Murry

Katherine Mansfield and John Middleton Murry rented The Gables at Cholesbury for a short spell before the First World War. The couple also later lived at Rose Tree Cottage in The Lee, a pretty village some three miles away.

New Zealand-born Katherine wrote short stories and is best remembered for *The Garden Party*. Murry was a successful critic and edited a number of publications.

The Gables is situated close to the famous windmill, which stands on the Cholesbury-Hawridge border.

Gilbert Cannan

Novelist Gilbert Cannan made his home at the picturesque Cholesbury Mill. The windmill still dominates the local skyline and attracts curious sightseers from the nearby pub.

The Cannans lived in their converted mill house during the First World War. It became a meeting place for members of the famous Bloomsbury Group, which included both writers and artists. Lytton Strachey and Dora Carrington were particularly close friends.

Gilbert Cannan was a highly regarded novelist in his time, but little remembered as a man of letters today. His spouse, Mary, was the former wife of J.M. Barrie.

HYDE HEATH

Benjamin Disraeli

Benjamin Disraeli is reputed to have penned most of *Vivian Grey* at Hyde House. Father Isaac D'Israeli rented the property for a spell in the 1820s when he was looking for a house in the country for a few weeks.

The large residence, with a long, straight drive fronting onto the main road between Chesham and Great Missenden, belonged to politician Robert Plumer Ward, the author of *Tremaine*, which is said to have inspired *Vivian Grey*.

The now-forgotten former Poet Laureate Henry James Pye can claim to be the one who first introduced the Disraelis to the Chiltern area. Having fallen on hard

Cholesbury Mill was home to Gilbert Cannan.

Hyde House, where Benjamin Disraeli wrote Vivian Grey.

times, Pye had been provided with a cottage near Stoke Poges by John Penn, grandson of Quaker and pioneer William Penn. Through Pye, Isaac D'Israeli became a guest of Penn and got to know the area well. He was obviously impressed with the region and eventually decided to move to the Chilterns on a permanent basis. Isaac told Robert Southey, another guest of Penn at Stoke Poges: 'The precarious health of several members of my family has decided me upon this movement, and I quit London with all its hourly seductions.'

The family moved to Bradenham, though Hughenden was later to become the property most associated with the Disraelis.

LATIMER

Thomas Fuller

Thomas Fuller, author of *Worthies of England*, immortalised a very worthy and productive resident of Buckinghamshire.

Hester Sandys, who is believed to have been born in the village of Latimer and baptised in Chesham, produced – according to the writer – four sons and nine daughters following her marriage to Thomas Temple of Stowe. That was not so unusual in the seventeenth century, but all the children survived infancy, married, and 'so exceedingly multiplied that this lady saw 700 extracted from her body'. Fuller added: 'Reader, I speak within compass, and have left myself a reserve, having bought the truth hereof by a wager I lost.'

Horace Walpole

The impressive manor house at Latimer did not do much for Horace Walpole. He was a regular visitor to the area and wrote much about many places in the neighbourhood, including Latimer House, which sits in a fine position on a hill above the River Chess.

But Walpole, who stayed here on a number of occasions in the eighteenth century, was not easily pleased and wrote: 'The view is melancholy.'

Latimer House is now a conference centre. You can judge the view yourself, as the Chess Valley Walk footpath runs alongside the property. It was not the only house in the area to fall foul of the writer . . .

CHENIES

Horace Walpole

Horace Walpole was even less impressed with Chenies Manor. He described it as being in a state of dilapidation when he visited. He did take a shine to some of the neglected windows, however, commenting on the 'beautiful arms in painted glass', adding that he wished to have them for Strawberry Hill. Walpole was forever scouring the country in search of new things to furnish his Twickenham home.

Antiquary John Leland saw Chenies in a better light when he came in the sixteenth century and described the property in glowing terms. Beautiful Chenies Manor is certainly not neglected these days. It is open for at least two days a week during the summer months and is blessed with an enchanting garden.

James Anthony Froude

Historian James Anthony Froude came to Chenies in 1879. Chenies Manor has been the home of the Russell family, the earls and dukes of Bedford, for centuries. Froude, a Tory, following his visit here, mocked the famous Whig family through his pen, claiming that all was 'old-fashioned, grave and respectable'.

His article on Chenies and the house of Russell first appeared in *Fraser's Magazine*, the famous periodical Froude had earlier edited. It was later reprinted in *Short Studies on Great Subjects*.

Another visitor at the end of the nineteenth century was Virginia Woolf. She was a child when she stayed at Chenies Manor with her family. Virginia later recalled visiting the ancient parish church where the dukes of Bedford are buried.

Miles Coverdale

The great Bible translator and bishop was domestic chaplain to the Russell family for a few years in the middle of the sixteenth century. Visitors to Chenies Manor can view the room that was supposedly set aside for the use of the family's chaplains.

Coverdale was one of the most prominent Protestant reformers. He was responsible for the first complete Bible to be printed in English.

A number of Elizabethan poets would have also graced Chenies. Lucy Harington became the Countess of Bedford after her marriage to Edward Russell, the 3rd Earl of Bedford, in 1594.

Virginia Woolf visited Chenies Manor at the end of the nineteenth century.

As a courtier and patron of the arts, she entertained some of the leading scribes of the day at her various properties, one of which was Chenies, the home of the Russells.

Michael Drayton, Samuel Daniel, John Donne and Ben Jonson were among her associates. Donne, in particular, wrote several poems in her honour. It has also been claimed that William Shakespeare may have penned *A Midsummer Night's Dream* for the couple's wedding.

AMERSHAM

John Wycliffe

Protestant reformer and Bible translator John Wycliffe became the inspiration for the lives and deaths of many. Buckinghamshire was a particular stronghold for his followers, with many meeting in secret to study his work, which included an English translation of the Bible.

The Lollards, the name given to those that began to spread the ideas of Wycliffe, first met in Oxford and the movement expanded east to the Chilterns. Wycombe, Chesham, Chalfont and particularly Amersham were especially active in helping to spark the flame of the Protestant Reformation, which was eventually to follow.

Wycliffe and the Lollards, who published many tracts to get across their views, attacked abuses in the Church and the authority of priests. It was the beginning of the end for Roman Catholicism in England, but there was to be much suffering before the battle was won. The Lollards were labelled heretics. The Church was of the belief that the word of God was sacred, and considered translation of the Scriptures to be heresy.

Amersham had more than its fair share of martyrs. The deaths of seven men and women are recorded on a stone obelisk, known as the Martyrs' Memorial, which stands almost hidden on a hill overlooking the town. A footpath from Station Road leads to the spot. William Tylsworth was among the seven. Cruelly, his married daughter was forced to start the fire that was to end the life of this brave Christian, who 'died for the principles of religious liberty'. His execution, which is recorded in John Foxe's famous *Acts and Monuments*, took place in 1506, more than 100 years after the death of Wycliffe. It provided further evidence that the reformer's ideas could not be repressed and had only gathered momentum over the years.

The Martyrs' Memorial at Amersham.

William Penn

Amersham appealed to William Penn, or at least a certain resident did.

The area, as we have seen through the Lollards, was a particular stronghold for dissenters. In the seventeenth century, it was the Quakers who fought for religious freedom.

Penn was a new convert to the faith and would regularly visit the home of Quakers Isaac and Mary Penington. In fact, it was Mrs Penington and Gulielma Springett, a daughter from her first marriage, who first came to live in the town in the mid-1660s. Mr Penington was spending a spell behind bars for his beliefs and the two women could no longer afford to live on their own at the Grange in Chalfont St Peter, the family home. They had been turned out of their house and, after a short period in a property at Chalfont St Giles, moved to larger lodgings in what is now Old Amersham. Fellow Quaker and close friend Thomas Ellwood found Bury House for them. Bury Farm is situated at the foot of Gore Hill on the road to Coleshill.

Penn soon fell in love with Gulielma, the woman who would often be seen crossing the fields to Chalfont St Giles with a lute in her hand for the benefit of the blind John Milton, the latter having taken up residence there. Penn and Guli, as she was affectionately known, eventually married at Chorleywood in 1672 and set up home in Rickmansworth.

The Peningtons are thought to have later lived in various places in the area, such as Woodside Farm. It was one of a number of farms that existed on Amersham Common before the area was developed as Amersham-on-the-Hill. Some of the old farm buildings now form part of the present community centre.

Isaac Penington, after various spells in prison, is believed to have spent his final few years in relative peace at Amersham.

The town and surrounding area was a stronghold for Quakerism. An incident in 1665 highlighted the fact that the Quakers suffered almost as much persecution as the Lollards, in both life and death. During the funeral of a prominent Amersham Quaker, which Penington and his friends were attending, a passing magistrate, unprovoked, struck one of the bearers and the coffin fell to the ground. The man of law ordered the arrest of all the mourners and the body lay in the street all day until the authorities finally buried it in an unconsecrated corner of the churchyard. The incident is recorded in *The History of the Life of Thomas Ellwood – Written by Himself*. Ellwood, like Penn, was a prolific man of letters.

George Fox – founder of the Quakers – is believed to have been a regular visitor to the area. His literary fame rests on his *Journal*, which describes his incredible spiritual journey.

Richard Baxter

Eminent Puritan divine Richard Baxter, author of *The Saint's Everlasting Rest*, was among those who battled against the spread of Quakerism. He preached in Amersham and all over the area. He recorded: 'The countries about Rickmansworth abounding with Quakers, because Mr W. Penn their captain, dwelleth there, I was desirous that the poor people should once hear what was to be said for their recovery.'

John Knox

Scottish Puritan and reformer John Knox came to the town a century earlier and sparked even more controversy. Knox, on a preaching tour of Buckinghamshire in 1553, arrived in Amersham from London and addressed a large and mostly hostile congregation. It is said things became so heated, troops were called to quell the disturbances that occurred following the service.

Thomas Hooker

Thomas Hooker, another famous Puritan minister, enjoyed a happier reception at Amersham. He married Susannah Garbrand at St Mary's Church in 1621. She was the niece of Dr Robert Chaloner, the rector of Amersham and founder of the town's famous 'free grammar school'. Dr Challoner's School, (now spelt with an extra 'l'), still exists in Amersham-on-the-Hill. Hooker wrote a number of religious works.

Thomas Hooker was wed at St Mary's Church.

George Orwell

Novelist George Orwell knew this part of the country well. In his most famous dystopian novel, *Nineteen Eighty-Four*, Parsons's young daughter persuades two others in her troop to slip off from their Saturday hike in the Berkhamsted area to follow a stranger and possible spy. 'They kept on his tail for two hours, right through the woods, and then, when they got into Amersham, handed him over to the patrols.'

COLESHILL

Edmund Waller

The village of Coleshill was the birthplace of Edmund Waller, a once popular writer who lived through the troubled days of the Civil War.

Waller was born at Stock Place at the beginning of the seventeenth century. It is believed the family moved to nearby Beaconsfield while the author was of a young age, so the romantic notion of him penning his poems in the hollow of a large tree here – later known as Waller's Oak – may be just that, unless he was in the habit of regularly making the short trip back to his former home.

Waller was baptised at Amersham and served the town as an MP at the age of just 16. Though he lived most of his life at Beaconsfield, he never forgot his childhood abode and it remained his first love. Towards the end of his life, the poet longed to return to the place of his birth. He said: 'A stag, when he is hunted, and near spent, always returns home.' Unfortunately, this particular one did not and he was buried at Beaconsfield following his death.

Stock Place has much changed. It is now one of a number of private houses in Manor Way, which stand on the former estate. Another is called 'Waller's Oak', after the famous tree now within its back garden.

Children's author and novelist Laurence Meynell lived in 'Waller's Oak' for a spell in the 1950s before moving to the Great Missenden area and then on to Brighton.

Thomas Ellwood

Quaker poet Thomas Ellwood spent the final part of his life at Coleshill. He moved here with wife Mary Ellis, a local girl, whom he wed in 1669. They lived in a small farmhouse called Hunger Hill (now Ongar Hill) just off Magpie Lane. Ellwood died here in 1713. The actual house no longer exists.

Much of what we know about the author and his fellow Quakers is gleaned from his autobiography, *The History of the Life of Thomas Ellwood – Written by Himself.*

He also wrote religious tracts and poems. He is best known for the poem *Davideis*, a piece on King David, and for his part in editing the journal of George Fox, the founder of the Quakers.

Ellwood was born at Crowell just over the border in Oxfordshire and lived much of his early life with the Peningtons, a famous Quaker family, at Chalfont St Peter.

6

Beacon for the Rich and Famous

Beaconsfield and its surrounding villages have long been associated with wealth and affluence. One recent survey heralded the area as the most expensive place to live in England. The prosperous and successful continue to make their home here, as did many men and women of letters before them. In fact, few towns the size of Beaconsfield can claim so many literary connections.

Other scribes, such as John Milton, came to the area through necessity, while many of his Quaker friends provide evidence that not all who made their home here were welcomed with open arms.

BEACONSFIELD

Edmund Waller

A stone obelisk in the churchyard at Beaconsfield marks the resting place of Edmund Waller. His wish to return home to nearby Coleshill, the place of his birth, did not come to fruition and he died at Hall Barn, his second home in the Chilterns.

Hall Barn at Windsor End was – and still is – a grand estate, though Waller was away from it for long spells because of the political problems of the time. The poet sought to steer a moderate course during the problematic 1640s. He was a distant relative of Oliver Cromwell and cousin of John Hampden, but, in 1643, was imprisoned in the Tower for his part in a Royalist plot to oust the Parliamentarians. The writer used his considerable charm and guile to escape death, but was fined and exiled. On his return, he tried to regain Cromwell's favour and wrote a panegyric poem in his honour.

Famously, following the Restoration, Charles II became the subject matter for another glowing tribute. The king was no fool, however, and questioned why the work in honour of him was not as good as that devoted to Cromwell many years earlier. The sharp-witted Waller replied: 'Sir, we poets never succeed so well in writing truth as in fiction.' Many claimed Waller was the personification of Mr Facing-both-ways in John Bunyan's *The Pilgrim's Progress*.

*The extravagant tomb
of Edmund Waller.*

Waller is best remembered for the verse *Go, Lovely Rose*. He was one of the greatest lyric poets the country has ever produced, but few of his poems have survived the test of time.

It is thought that Waller built the original Hall Barn some time between 1675 and 1687, the year of his death. The house today, though much changed over the years, has been returned to as close to the original structure as possible. Its lavish grounds, complete with an obelisk and ornamental statues, are only occasionally open to the public. The parish church also contains memorials to members of Waller's family. Diarist John Evelyn came to Beaconsfield and called Hall Barn 'Waller's town box'.

William Hickey

Diarist William Hickey came to Beaconsfield in the early nineteenth century. He took a pretty cottage called Little Hall Barn, which still stands in Windsor End, close to Hall Barn.

Hickey gained fame for his adventures in India. The entertaining *Memoirs of William Hickey* recount his travels, life as a lawyer and his weakness for women and wine.

Edmund Burke

Biographer John Morley wrote that it was a 'touching picture to the historic imagination' to follow Edmund Burke 'from the heat and violence of the House, where tipsy squires derided the greatest genius of his time, down to the calm shades of Beaconsfield'. And it is not difficult to imagine the celebrated statesman and writer

Hall Barn, 'Waller's town box'.

Little Hall Barn was home to William Hickey.

pacing the walk of his impressive mansion, reflecting on 'the state of Europe and the distractions of his country'.

Burke purchased Gregories in 1768 and renamed it Butler's Court. It remained his retreat from the pressures of Parliament until his death in 1797. Forever plagued by debt, he still had a mortgage of £14,000 to pay when he died.

Burke was a rash man. Financially, the purchase of this rather pretentious mansion was a mistake and left him in debt for the rest of his life, but he loved his home and refused to give it up. He perilously maintained the estate, despite threats of warrants and visits from impatient bailiffs. Burke was never really bothered by money matters. On one occasion, a solicitor was instructed to serve a writ on him and arrived at Butler's Court. As he approached the house, he asked a man ploughing an adjoining field if Mr Burke was at home. The man told him he was out and the solicitor left. That ploughman was Burke himself.

Though always in financial difficulty, Burke was a generous and caring man. His politics defended the cause of civil justice and he was a champion of the needy. He was a politician who believed in action and not just words. Morley described Burke giving food to beggars with his own hands.

Burke loved Beaconsfield and liked nothing more than walking in the surrounding woods or working his land. He was also fond of entertaining. Among his literary guests were Samuel Johnson, Richard Brinsley Sheridan, Arthur Murphy and David Garrick.

Despite his political and literary success, the politician and philosopher ended his life a sad man following the death of his only son. Burke, who is best known for *Reflections on the Revolution in France*, was buried in St Mary & All Saints' Church, where there is a memorial.

Butler's Court was destroyed by fire in 1813, though there are many reminders of its existence, including a school named in its honour. The present house of that name was built on a different site towards the end of the nineteenth century.

Poet George Crabbe tested the generosity of Edmund Burke to the limit – and the latter was not found wanting. The statesman opened up his home to the debt-ridden young man and not only rescued him from the threat of prison, but also introduced him to his influential friends and helped to publish his poetry. It is thought that Crabbe spent the summer of 1781 at Butler's Court. It gave him time to get back on his feet and work on the poem that was to make his name – *The Village*.

G.K. Chesterton

The sight of Gilbert Keith Chesterton at his favourite spot beside the bar in the White Hart in debate with anyone brave enough to take on this man of words was a common one. There was nothing more the author liked than a chat at his favourite haunt.

Chesterton was a flamboyant and larger-than-life character, always full of energy, and he certainly made his mark in Beaconsfield. The town became his home for the last twenty-seven years or so of his life. He and his wife discovered it by accident, however. They set off one day from their London home without any idea where they might end up. At a railway ticket office, they asked where the next train was going. It was Slough. From there, they walked through the beechwoods and came upon

Beaconsfield and the White Hart. Both decided it was the place they wanted to live, though Mrs Chesterton was the keener of the two.

Chesterton was really a city man, but he certainly fell in love with the area and quickly integrated into the community. His sharp wit and sense of humour were highlighted during the First World War, when a local woman asked why he was not 'out at the front'. Chesterton, a vast figure of a man, replied: 'If you come round to the side, madam, you will see that I am!'

The Chestertons came to Beaconsfield in 1909. Overroads was the name of their first house in Grove Road, though they moved to Top Meadow, just across the road, in 1922, when building work on their second home was complete.

One of the most influential guests at Grove Road was Father John O'Connor. The Roman Catholic priest from Yorkshire was a close friend and became the inspiration for Father Brown, the author's famous detective.

The Catholic Church was greatly responsible for the direction Chesterton's pen took. The author was received into the faith fourteen years before his death. Beaconsfield's Catholic church at the time was a hall that formed part of the Railway Hotel, later known as The Earl of Beaconsfield, which no longer exists. Father O'Connor was among those who witnessed his friend being received into the faith, but, in truth, Chesterton was a Catholic long before that official reception, as his writing, which was mostly of a devotional nature, suggests.

A new Catholic church was built in 1926 and is perhaps the finest memorial to Chesterton in Beaconsfield. The Church of St Teresa is situated opposite Bekonscot Model Village in New Town. Many artefacts in the church are associated with its

Top Meadow, home of G.K. Chesterton.

G.K. Chesterton frequented the White Hart (left) and is buried in Beaconsfield's cemetery (below).

most famous parishioner. Building was finally completed after Chesterton's death as a memorial to him, thanks to the generosity of his friends and many admirers from around the world.

In his final years, Chesterton became saddened by the many growing changes to the Chiltern area, with more and more agricultural land being sold for the development of new estates. He fought hard to keep this development within bounds.

Chesterton was buried at the cemetery in Shepherds Lane. The crucifix on the gravestone is the work of famous sculptor and writer Eric Gill.

Novelist Angela Thirkell was among those that stayed at Top Meadow following the death of G.K. Chesterton. Dorothy Collins, the writer's secretary, first ran it as a home for unmarried mothers and later took in paying guests as well. It was Chesterton's wish that the property should be used for religious purposes, which became the case. Angela Thirkell's novels depict an idealised country life and she saw Beaconsfield as the perfect model. The town features in a number of her works.

Enid Blyton

The Beaconsfield home of Enid Blyton became one of the best-known houses in the country. Children only needed to address their fan mail to 'Green Hedges, England' for it to reach its destination, and young fans would come from far and wide to get the author's autograph. It is easy to picture excited children standing on the doorstep, their gaze fixed on the small Noddy figures that once graced the front garden.

Sadly, Green Hedges, the house where Enid spent the final thirty years of her life, no longer stands and the only evidence sightseers will find today is a street name in her honour. The houses in Blyton Close, a cul-de-sac, now sit on the site of her former residence and its large garden.

The family moved to Beaconsfield from nearby Bourne End in 1938. The name given to the large detached property in Penn Road was the idea of Enid's young readers. Children were invited to choose a name for the author's new abode and 'Green Hedges' won by a large majority. Enid wrote many of her most famous works here, including *Five on a Treasure Island* and *Noddy Goes to Toyland*.

While her literary career blossomed at Green Hedges, Enid's personal life was not so enriching. Her husband, Hugh Pollock, was away from home for much of the war and their marriage suffered as a result. The couple were to eventually divorce and Enid went on to spend much time in London, taking a lease on a flat that became the meeting point for her and Kenneth Darrell Waters, who was later to become her second husband.

Enid and Kenneth could often be seen playing golf at the local course in Beaconsfield, while Green Hedges became the venue for a number of grand dinner parties, with many eminent locals and publishers among the guests.

Enid would spend most days sitting in a chair on the veranda, her typewriter resting on a plank laid across her knees. The author's most prolific writing years were between 1949 and 1952. It is thought that she penned one of her 'Famous Five' novels in less than a week. Taking into account that the average length of the works was somewhere between 40,000 and 50,000 words, she probably produced about 1,500 words an hour if she worked a full day.

Enid would often spend the day locked in her own imagination, sometimes oblivious to the world around her. Her character is not always seen in a good light these days, however. Even her daughter Imogen depicted a miserable childhood at Green Hedges in her memoirs, claiming her mother was too busy to give her the attention she needed. It is ironic that the author should bring so much pleasure to children throughout the world, but have been accused of perhaps neglecting her own offspring in doing so.

Indeed, in her final lonely days, following the death of her second husband, Enid was told that she could at least take comfort in her children. She is reportedly to have drawn attention to the large bookcase with her many works on it and said: 'Children. These are my children.'

Enid died of Alzheimer's disease in a nursing home in Hampstead in 1968, a year after the death of her second husband.

Alison Uttley

Another children's author lived in Beaconsfield at the same time as Enid Blyton.

Alison Uttley gained fame for her *Little Grey Rabbit* books. The author moved to Beaconsfield in 1938 – the same year as Enid Blyton – and lived here for the rest of her life. It is thought the two children's writers did not get on.

Though she was born in the Peak District, Alison knew Buckinghamshire from earlier visits to Chesham Bois and the country home of her friend, Ramsay MacDonald, who went on to become prime minister on three seperate occasions.

Thackers – the name Alison gave to her new home – is situated in Ellwood Road. Alison had a number of literary friends, including Walter de la Mare, whom she visited at nearby Penn, the village in which she herself now lies at rest.

Robert Frost

American Robert Frost was unknown and unpublished when he came to Beaconsfield in 1912. Though he only stayed for some eighteen months, it proved to be an important and productive period in his life.

The family left the United States in order to spend a couple of years in England, where Frost could devote more time to his writing. It proved to be a wise move.

He rented a cottage in Reynolds Road. The Bungalow, as it was called, no longer exists, but a plaque now marks the spot where it stood. It was here that Frost enjoyed his literary breakthrough. *A Boy's Will*, his first book of poems, was published in 1913. *North of Boston*, which contains the famous *Mending Wall*, *Home Burial* and *After Apple-picking*, followed the next year.

Though the family moved to Gloucestershire in 1914, and, subsequently, back to the United States, Frost did visit Beaconsfield in later years, such was the affection he held for the town.

Rose Macaulay

Novelist and essayist Rose Macaulay was another Beaconsfield resident. She lived at Hedgerley End in Hedgerley Lane. Her novels include *The World My Wilderness* and *The Towers of Trebizond*, both of which appeared in print in the 1950s.

*Poet Robert Frost lived
in Beaconsfield.*

PENN

Edmund Burke

The archetypal English village of Penn is perhaps the last place you would expect to hear the sound of foreign accents. But if you had come here at the end of the eighteenth century, it would have been quite a different story.

French School Meadows in Elm Road is the only reminder today of the educational establishment set up by writer and MP Edmund Burke in the mid-1790s. The roomy house where dozens of orphans of the French Revolution dwelt has long gone.

Burke, who lived at nearby Beaconsfield, was a well-known sympathiser of the French émigrés. His house was always open to exiles from France, and guests included Louis XVIII and other members of the royal family who came to offer their thanks for all that he had done for them.

The school at Penn, set up in a house that once belonged to General William Haviland, whose monument can be found in the parish church, was for the sons or relatives of French gentlemen killed during the Revolution. The sight of up to sixty blue-coated boys proudly marching in military array through the lanes of Penn must have been a bizarre one. The youngsters wore caps with inscriptions that revealed Burke's politics. The words 'Vive le Roi' (Long Live the King) were written in red if the child's father had fallen in battle.

Burke was much loved by all at the school. The children, and even some of the teachers, saw him as a second father. He was a generous man and would often go without things himself in order to bring a few luxuries to his new 'sons'. Others were not so enamoured with the whole idea, however, and Burke struggled to maintain the charity. He publicly criticised dukes, marquises, cabinet ministers and other politicians of the day who were less reluctant to offer support to the school. 'Cannot this miserable little affair of fifty pounds a month be done between them?' he raged on one occasion when the matter of funding was being considered in Parliament.

Burke gained fame for the treatise *Reflections on the Revolution in France*, which was published in 1790.

The exact location of Burke's school is not known, but Penn & Tylers Green Football Club are believed to now occupy the site, the club's home ground being called French School Meadows. The blue uniform and white feathers worn in the pupils' caps inspired the club's blue and white colours, as well as their crest.

William Penn

It is thought that Quaker William Penn, founder of Pennsylvania, America, never actually lived in Penn. There is even some doubt as to whether his ancestors, who took their name from the village, were those that now lay at rest in the parish church. But Penn, who made such a mark with his pen, certainly believed this secluded village to be his ancestral home. He was convinced he was a Penn of Penn!

Holy Trinity Church has several monuments to the Penn family and, though Penn himself is buried at nearby Jordans, some of his grandchildren are also buried in the vaults here.

Penn was the child of a leading naval commander. The son, much to his father's disgust, became a Quaker and spent most of his life in a battle to win religious freedom for all. Penn became a prolific writer on the faith. His best-known literary work is *No Cross, No Crown*, which he wrote while imprisoned in the Tower. He was to spend much time behind bars because of his beliefs.

Penn has many links with the Chiltern area, but his legacy is stronger in America. Charles II owed Penn's father a debt and so granted the son land in the New World. Penn set sail and named it Pennsylvania, establishing it as a place of religious liberty.

The Quakers refused to remove their hats and Penn famously kept his on in the presence of Charles II. The king graciously removed his own, as it was custom for only one person at a time to remain covered.

Holy Trinity Church is full of history and has become a place of pilgrimage for those now living in the land established by the most famous Penn of all.

Walter de la Mare

Poet Walter de la Mare stayed at Old Park in Hammersley Lane for much of the Second World War and beyond. Though his main home from 1940 until his death was in Twickenham, he would spend long periods here. He was a prolific writer of poems, short stories and novels, including *Memoirs of a Midget* (1921).

Alison Uttley

Children's author Alison Uttley is buried in the pretty churchyard at Penn. Her simple gravestone sums up her craft. The inscription reads: 'A spinner of tales.'

Alison Uttley, who died in 1976, is thought to have first visited Walter de la Mare at Old Park in 1940. The two writers became great friends. She was a regular worshipper at Holy Trinity Church, often cycling to services from her Beaconsfield home. Her grave is located in the churchyard extension close to the church cross.

Above: *The Penns lie at rest in Holy Trinity Church.*

Right: *Alison Uttley is buried at Penn.*

George Grove

The Grove family have long been associated with Penn. Family residences in the village included Stonehouse and Watercroft, which are both situated in Church Road.

George Grove, a writer on music, was the most famous member of the family. His reputation today rests on his *Dictionary of Music and Musicians*, a voluminous work that first appeared in the late 1870s.

John Betjeman called Penn 'the Chelsea of the Chilterns'. He believed it had retained its own identity despite its close proximity to High Wycombe.

CHALFONT ST GILES

John Milton

The great John Milton never really saw the 'pretty box' he lived in for a short spell towards the end of his life. It is thought the writer was almost totally blind when he came to Chalfont St Giles to escape the London plague in 1665. He stayed for less than a year.

The delightful cottage, the only building that Milton lived in that still survives, is indeed a picture, and many visitors flock to set eyes on it themselves.

The author came in the summer and, because of his blindness, was mostly confined to the garden where he would sit enjoying the afternoon sun, clad in his favourite coarse grey suit. It was close friend and former pupil, Thomas Ellwood who found the cottage for him. In *The History of the Life of Thomas Ellwood – Written by Himself*, the Quaker wrote:

> I was desired by my quondam master, Milton, to take a house for him in the neighbourhood where I dwelt, that he might go out of the city, for the safety of himself and his family, the pestilence then growing hot in London. I took a pretty box for him in Giles Chalfont, a mile from me.

Ellwood was staying at the Chalfont St Peter home of his great friends Isaac and Mary Penington at the time. Unfortunately, he did not have the pleasure of greeting his former master at his new home, as Ellwood was serving a spell at Aylesbury Gaol when Milton arrived. It was not the first or the last time the passionate Quaker would suffer for his beliefs.

Milton might not have been able to see his new home, but it is likely he knew the area. He lived at Horton, near Windsor, for a spell in the 1630s and regularly enjoyed rambles into this part of the country. Milton also endured the winter at Chalfont St Giles, only returning to London in the early spring of 1666, when it was considered safe to do so.

Ellwood, on his release from prison, eventually visited the poet at the house he had found for him. The former informs us in his autobiography that Milton had handed him the completed manuscript of *Paradise Lost*. The Quaker wrote: 'He asked me how I liked it and what I thought of it, which I modestly but freely told him, and, after some further discourse about it, I pleasantly said to him, "thou hast said much here of Paradise Lost, but what hast thou to say of Paradise Found?"' Ellwood said Milton

John Milton's 'pretty box' at Chalfont St Giles.

made no answer, but 'sat some time in a muse' before changing the subject. Some time later, when Milton was back in London, he handed Ellwood the manuscript of *Paradise Regained*, the sequel to his greatest work, and said: 'This is owing to you, for you put it into my head by the question you put to me at Chalfont.'

Milton's Cottage, as it is now known, is open to the public throughout the summer.

CHALFONT ST PETER

Thomas Ellwood
The Grange at Chalfont St Peter was home to Isaac and Mary Penington. The Peningtons were influential Quakers and close friends of writer Thomas Ellwood.

The latter considered the Peningtons his spiritual parents following his conversion to the faith, which is recorded in *The History of the Life of Thomas Ellwood – Written by Himself*. The author tells us he came to inform the family of his decision to become a Quaker, only to find their daughter, Gulielma, ill with smallpox at the time. The Peningtons were concerned that their guest might catch the disease, but Ellwood said he was too excited to worry about it. Ellwood stayed at the Grange for long periods.

Horace Walpole
Man of letters Horace Walpole was a regular visitor to Chalfont Park. He came here after his half-sister married the owner of the estate, Charles Churchill, who should not be confused with the poet of the same name. Walpole mentions Chalfont Park in a number of his writings. Chalfont Park House is now used as a business premises.

Horace Walpole visited Chalfont Park House.

JORDANS

The Quakers

Step inside the Quaker Meeting House at Jordans and you will not have much difficulty picturing the likes of Thomas Ellwood and William Penn sitting in silent prayer. Many a time they would have come and gone from this quaint setting, decked in their wide-brimmed hats.

It is here that Ellwood and Penn are also laid to rest. The simple burial ground outside contains the graves of many of their fellow believers too, including members of their own families and close friends, Isaac and Mary Penington.

Jordans may not have been home to the first Quaker Meeting House, but it is probably the most famous. The village attracts many visitors from America, and Pennsylvania in particular, who are keen to pay homage to William Penn, the founder of the state.

The Quaker Meeting House at Jordans was built in 1688, following James II's Declaration of Indulgence that sought freedom of worship for Catholics, but which also benefited Quakers and other dissenters.

The believers met here much earlier, however, but in secret. George Fox, the founder of the Quakers, is thought to have come to Jordans on a number of occasions when meetings were held at the old farmhouse, now a hotel.

The Mayflower Barn also attracts the tourists. It is believed timbers from the famous ship of the same name that carried the Pilgrim Fathers to New England were used in its construction.

The Quaker Meeting House contains Quaker memorabilia, including works of Ellwood and Penn, who were both prolific writers. Sadly, a major restoration project had to be undertaken in 2005 after a serious fire.

William Penn is buried at Jordans.

GERRARDS CROSS

John Betjeman

Poet John Betjeman spent a short spell teaching at Thorpe House School in Oval Way, Gerrards Cross. He came here following his studies at Oxford.

Betjeman went on to write much about Buckinghamshire and its surrounding counties. He loved the area – but not all of it. He famously suggested it would be a good idea to drop bombs on Slough in neighbouring Berkshire.

Horace Walpole – a regular visitor at nearby Chalfont – also came to Bulstrode Park, a centre for intellectuals and statesmen during the eighteenth century. He was not impressed, however. 'I have been often at Bulstrode from Chalfont, but I don't like it,' he once declared.

Captain Mayne Reid, a nineteenth-century writer who gained fame for his adventure novels, lived in Gerrards Cross for a spell.

DENHAM

John Dryden

Poet John Dryden was a frequent visitor to Denham Court, the home of relatives. The mansion in Dryden's time (the present house is now home to a golf club), was an impressive property and the poet called its garden 'one of the most delicious in England'. It is said he penned *A Song for St Cecilia's Day* here in the late 1680s.

Samuel Johnson was among other men of letters to have stayed within the walls of Denham Court.

IVER

Alexander Pope

Alexander Pope was one of many literary visitors to the grand mansion that once stood here. Richings Park, now a purpose-built residential development, was once the estate of politician Lord Bathurst, who entertained most of the literary greats of the eighteenth century. Pope, who enjoyed long walks in the area, addressed his host in *Epistle to Bathurst*.

STOKE POGES

Thomas Gray

Perhaps the most inappropriate shrine to a writer is the one dedicated to poet Thomas Gray. Gray, the reason so many people make a pilgrimage to the Buckinghamshire village of Stoke Poges, was the last person who wanted to draw attention to himself. During his lifetime, he shunned fame and was not at all ambitious. Few poets have gained so many plaudits by publishing so little.

Gray's Monument, a massive and intimidating sarcophagus, was designed by architect James Wyatt and placed in the field (now Gray's Field) next to the church where the poet based his most famous work. It was the idea of John Penn of nearby Stoke Park, the grandson of pioneer and Quaker William Penn, and was erected at the end of the eighteenth century. His intentions were honourable and there should indeed be a memorial to this great of English literature, but perhaps the best tribute is the churchyard itself, where this shy poet now lies and where he penned one of the most famous poems in the English language.

Tourists can sometimes be seen with a copy of *Elegy Written in a Country Churchyard* in their hands as they sit where the author himself sat to write it, under the yew tree that still shades the porch of St Giles. Gray started writing the poem in the mid-1740s. He altered it from time to time, but did not actually complete it until 1750. It was published the following year.

The poet resided at West End House, now Stoke Court, during vacations from London and Cambridge. It was originally the home of his uncle, Jonathan Rogers. Following the latter's death in 1742, Gray's mother and another sister moved in with the poet's widowed aunt.

Gray strolled in the surrounding meadows and spent many an afternoon in the churchyard watching the sun go down. The poet was content with the beautiful countryside around him and wrote: 'I have, at the distance of half a mile, through a green lane, a forest (the vulgar call it a common) all my own, at least as good as so, for I spy no human thing in it but myself.'

Gray never married, but, despite his shyness, was not an unsociable man. It is believed he had only one love and there is some doubt it got any further than just a friendship. Close to West End House sat a grand manor house, the home of Lady Cobham and her niece Henrietta Speed. Miss Speed and a friend one day made it their mission to befriend the reserved poet and so set off across the fields to call upon him. In truth, Gray, though a solitary man, was happy to accept their

*Thomas Gray's Monument
at Stoke Poges.*

friendship. It is thought he wrote *A Long Story* for them. The work is set at the manor house, which still stands close to the church, though it has much changed. John Penn demolished most of it and built the present mansion at Stoke Park, which is now home to a golf club. There are excellent views of both from the beautiful memorial gardens next to the church.

In the nineteenth century, the Penn family could not afford the upkeep of both the Manor House and West End. They sold the former and enlarged the latter, changing its name to Stoke Court. Thus, from a humble cottage, the former home of the Grays has become the mansion it is today. Stoke Court has been graced by a number of literary visitors over the years, including John Buchan, Thomas Hardy, Somerset Maugham and John Galsworthy. A private company now owns it. The manor house is also in private hands.

Visitors to the church often overlook Gray's final resting place. He is buried alongside his mother and one of his aunts. The poet wrote a simple memorial on his mother's headstone: 'The careful tender mother of many children, one of whom alone had the misfortune to survive her.' Only a plaque on the exterior wall of the church informs us that the son was also buried here, some eighteen years later. Following his mother's death in 1753, Gray was reluctant to return to Stoke Poges and he severed his ties with it completely after the death of his last relative here.

The churchyard where Thomas Gray wrote his elegy.

Aldous Huxley

Aldous Huxley drew upon the greatest work of Thomas Gray for an incident in his famous novel, *Brave New World*. In the futuristic work, first published in 1932, there is a golf course at Stoke Poges, where people go to play obstacle golf. Lenina and Henry are forced to abandon their game. Chapter five begins: 'The loud-speakers in the tower of the Stoke Poges Club House began, in a more than human tenor, to announce the closing of the courses.' The author is clearly making a witty reference to Gray's opening line of *Elegy Written in a Country Churchyard*, penned at Stoke Poges, which begins: 'The curfew tolls the knell of parting day.'

Other local places also get a mention in Huxley's sci-fi novel. Burnham Beeches stretches 'like a great pool of darkness' beneath the helicopter of Lenina and Henry, while the 'great factory' at Farnham Royal is another visible landmark in the fading light.

Aldous Huxley was not the only novelist to immortalise this part of the world . . .

FARNHAM COMMON

George Orwell

George Orwell sent Rosemary and Gordon to Farnham Common in *Keep the Aspidistra Flying*. They travelled here via 'an absurd chocolate-coloured bus with no top' and 'exclaimed at the loveliness of everything. The dew, the stillness, the satiny stems of the birches, the softness of the turf under your feet'!

Orwell knew the area well. He was educated at Eton and he later worked as a teacher at Hayes and Uxbridge in Middlesex. His literary agent also lived at Gerrards Cross and the author would make the journey on his motorbike.

Aldous Huxley knew Stoke Poges Club House.

FARNHAM ROYAL

Jacob Bryant

Antiquary and classical scholar Jacob Bryant loved reading so much, it ended up killing him! It is said he injured his leg while reaching for one of the books from his extensive library and developed a fatal infection.

It is believed Bryant was buried in the parish church at Farnham Royal, where there is a memorial plaque. He lived most of his later life at nearby Cippenham, where George III was among his visitors.

Though little remembered today, Bryant was one of the most respected scholars of the eighteenth century. He wrote works on a variety of subjects, many of which were of a religious interest.

Edward Chandler

It is said that, like Jacob Bryant, bishop and writer Edward Chandler is also buried at the Church of St Mary the Virgin in Farnham Royal. However, there is no memorial to the man who wrote much to protect the orthodox faith.

Chandler's most famous work is *Defence of Christianity*, which was published in 1725 in opposition to the controversial views of deist philosopher Anthony Collins.

EAST BURNHAM

George Grote

East Burnham Park provides evidence of the success of the most famous work of historian George Grote. Already a resident at East Burnham, Grote built the impressive house here through the profits of *History of Greece*. For this reason, it became known as the History Hut. The epic work was published over ten years, the first volume appearing in the mid-1840s.

Grote, a former politician and banker, entertained many illustrious guests at East Burnham over the years, including composer Felix Mendelssohn and singer Jenny Lind, both of whom enjoyed rambles at nearby Burnham Beeches.

Richard Brinsley Sheridan

Dramatist Richard Brinsley Sheridan came to East Burnham for his honeymoon. He brought singer and bride Elizabeth Linley to a cottage here after their ill-advised elopement in 1773.

The writer waxed lyrical about the surrounding area. He wrote: 'Were I in a descriptive vein, I would draw you some of the prettiest scenes imaginable. From my account of East Burnham you will say that Paradise was but a kitchen garden to it.'

Sheridan was another who delighted in Burnham Beeches, one of the most famous areas of woodland in the country.

BURNHAM BEECHES

Thomas Gray

Poet Thomas Gray used the word 'venerable' to describe the beeches that flourish in this part of the world. He also showed his love for the surroundings by immortalising them in his most famous work, *Elegy Written in a Country Churchyard*, which was penned at nearby Stoke Poges. In the poem, Gray refers to an old 'nodding beech' close to a brook. Sadly, the tree, which became known as 'Gray's beech', no longer exists, though visitors to Burnham Beeches will find a plaque close to the spot where it once stood, on the east side of the stream just north of the junction of Hawthorn Lane and Thompkins Lane.

Gray used to visit his uncle, Jonathan Rogers, at Cant's Hill, Burnham Grove. The latter would take him hunting, but the young scholar and lover of nature would prefer to sit under the beeches with a book in his hand. Mr and Mrs Rogers eventually moved to Stoke Poges, becoming leaseholders of West End House in 1739, which then became home to Gray's mother following the death of Mr Rogers in 1742.

BURNHAM

John Evelyn

Diarist John Evelyn stayed with relatives at Huntercombe Manor, now a hospital. He was full of praise for the building and beautiful gardens. Unlike the diary of contemporary Samuel Pepys, Evelyn's diary reveals little about the writer, but still offers a vital insight into seventeenth-century life.

Thomas Gray's 'nodding beech' once stood here.

7

Messing About in Boats

The Thames has been an inspiration to many for centuries. It straddles the bottom end of Buckinghamshire and serves as a natural border.

Our journey along the famous old river begins at Taplow and ends at Greenlands, the former home of a man who has left his mark on almost every major British high street.

Along the way, we will come across a diverse range of writers. A dreamy poet talked of revolution here, while his wife was busy creating a hideous and terrifying monster. And, of course, another scribe famously brought three men in a boat along here too . . . to say nothing of the dog.

TAPLOW

Julian Grenfell
Tragic First World War soldier-poet Julian Grenfell was the son of Lord Desborough, owner of impressive Taplow Court. Grenfell's most famous poem – *Into Battle* – was published on the day he was killed in 1915.

Lord Desborough (William Henry Grenfell) and his wife were themselves notable figures in Victorian society and Taplow Court was graced by many literary guests at the turn of the twentieth century, including Edith Wharton, Oscar Wilde and H.G. Wells.

H.G. Wells
Novelist H.G. Wells mentions Taplow Court in *Men Like Gods*. Taplow is also believed to be the place where the group are transported to and from the Utopian world at the beginning and end of the story.

Wells knew the Maidenhead and Windsor area very well. Places within the Thames Valley crop up in a number of his works.

Taplow Court has played host to many writers.

Walter de la Mare

Poet Walter de la Mare made Taplow his home from 1925 until the start of the Second World War. The writer lived at imposing Hill House at the top of Berry Hill at the junction with Rectory Road.

Charles Kingsley

Charles Kingsley, author of *The Water Babies*, was one visitor who could not conceal his delight over the landscape of this particular part of the Thames.

Kingsley, a clergyman who served the people of Eversley in Hampshire for most of his life, wrote: 'The most beautiful landscape I have ever seen or care to see is the vale of the Thames from Taplow or from Cliveden, looking down towards Windsor and up towards Reading.'

The author must have quite liked the locals too. He married Taplow-born Frances Grenfell.

Jerome K. Jerome

Jerome K. Jerome also liked what he saw beneath the steep wooded hills of Cliveden. He wrote: 'In its unbroken loveliness this is, perhaps, the sweetest stretch of all the river.' He tells us that 'Cliveden Woods still wore their dainty dress of spring' when the heroes of *Three Men in a Boat* – his most famous work – passed by.

Jerome loved the Thames and spent much of his life on or beside it. It is said he knew every stretch of the river before he was 30.

Hill House, home to Walter de la Mare.

Jerome K. Jerome loved Cliveden's steep wooded hills.

CLIVEDEN

James Thomson

Beautiful Cliveden has played host to many important people, including men of letters, over the years. Poet James Thomson was one of them. He co-wrote the masque *Alfred*, which was first performed at Cliveden in the 1740s, the house then belonging to Frederick, Prince of Wales. The work is famous for the patriotic song *Rule Britannia*, Thomson being responsible for the words. The Scottish poet gained fame for *The Seasons*, one of the most popular poems in the English language.

The house Thomson came to no longer exists, the present mansion being built in the nineteenth century.

George Villiers, 2nd Duke of Buckingham

Buckingham, a dramatist, is the man responsible for building the original house in the mid-seventeenth century. He was brought up in the royal household of Charles I and was constantly embroiled in the political troubles of the time. His greatest literary achievement is *The Rehearsal*, a burlesque play that mocked the heroic tragedy and did much to end that genre. The work satirised poet John Dryden in the person of Bayes. Dryden later gained his revenge by portraying Buckingham as Zimri in *Absalom and Achitophel*.

Cliveden became one of the homes of the famous Astor family. While in the hands of the 2nd Viscount Astor and his wife Nancy in the early twentieth century, like many great Buckinghamshire houses, it became an informal meeting place for men and women of letters. Henry James, Rudyard Kipling and Winston Churchill were among the frequent visitors.

HEDSOR

Nathaniel Hooke

The greatest achievement of historian Nathaniel Hooke has faded into obscurity. Hooke, who lies at rest in the parish churchyard, is said to have taken thirty years to complete the voluminous *Roman History*, which first appeared in 1738. Sadly for him, it was eclipsed by Edward Gibbon's *The History of the Decline and Fall of the Roman Empire*, which was published some forty years later.

Hooke is now more remembered as the lifelong friend of Alexander Pope than for his literary efforts, as great as they were.

BOURNE END

Enid Blyton

Readers of Enid Blyton have often sought in vain to find real locations in her many books. Bourne End, the author's home for most of the 1930s, is believed to be one place that did gain immortality in her famous stories for children. It is thought Peterswood in her 'Mystery' series was at least partly based on this large village on the Thames. There is plenty of evidence to support this claim. The stream flowing through Peterswood is called the Bourne and Enid reveals that Peterswood is in the county of Buckinghamshire. The author also states that Marlow is three miles from Peterswood, which just happens to be the distance between Marlow and Bourne End. Other local places, including Taplow and Burnham Beeches, also get a mention in the series.

It is not surprising Enid should choose to base Peterswood on Bourne End. She lived here for about nine years. She moved to Old Thatch, a large Tudor cottage in Coldmoorholme Lane, Well End, next to the Spade Oak pub, with first husband, Hugh Pollock in 1929. Its idyllic location, just a short walk from the Thames, was also enhanced by an extensive garden with an orchard, a small brook and an ancient well.

The couple moved here from Beckenham because they feared the growing development in that particular area. Enid wrote that 'a great new arterial road' was being planned in the neighbourhood.

The author enjoyed a cosseted lifestyle at Old Thatch, with a chauffeur-gardener, cook and housemaid to look after the family's needs. Enid would work at home in the day, but she was no hermit. She enjoyed socialising and would regularly be seen playing tennis during the long summer evenings.

One of her most famous creations at Bourne End was Bobs; a character based on her own dog. The author issued *Letters from Bobs* in 1933 and, within a week, some 10,000 copies of the booklet had been sold. Bobs actually died in 1935 and was buried in the garden at Old Thatch. The fact was concealed from readers, however, and Bobs continued 'writing' his letters for a few more years.

Old Thatch, the home of Enid Blyton.

Both of Enid's daughters were born while the couple were living at Bourne End, before the family moved to Beaconsfield in 1938.

The garden at Old Thatch is open to the public for a couple of days a week in the summer.

Edgar Wallace

The prolific Edgar Wallace had a house at Bourne End in the latter years of his life. Though he spent much of his time in Hollywood, where he died while working on the script for the blockbuster movie *King Kong*, his body was brought back to the area and laid here to rest.

Wallace was a versatile writer, but is chiefly remembered for his sensational thrillers. In 1928, at the height of his fame, it was said that one in four books being printed, excluding the Bible, were from his pen. It is reputed that Wallace could write a novel in three days.

Chalklands – the Bourne End home of the novelist – still stands in Blind Lane. It is now the base of a religious organisation and known as the Vedanta Centre. The grave of Wallace, who died in 1932, can be found in the cemetery at Fern Lane, Little Marlow.

MARLOW

Percy Bysshe Shelley

One can easily picture a thoughtful Percy Bysshe Shelley lying in a boat on the Thames where the 'interlaced branches mix and meet'. Jerome K. Jerome informs

Novelist Edgar Wallace lived at Chalklands.

us in *Three Men in a Boat* that 'it was while floating in his boat under the Bisham beeches' that Shelley composed *The Revolt of Islam*. The second stanza of the dedication of Shelley's work describes the river beside Quarry Wood where it was written.

Throughout the work and in a few other pieces he wrote at Marlow, Shelley refers to the surroundings he so fell in love with. But, on the whole, his imagination carried him further afield during those lazy afternoons beside or on the river. Marlow was perhaps the one place that Shelley, forever the wanderer, could call home. The eleven months he spent at Albion House were among his most happiest and productive.

The poet and his wife, Mary Shelley, moved into their new home in March 1817. They had married the previous December following the tragic suicide of Harriet, the poet's first wife. The couple hoped and intended that Albion House in West Street would become their home indefinitely. Shelley rented the pleasant but old-fashioned house on a long-term lease.

The poet enjoyed domestic bliss here, but it was a cold and damp property, which did not suit the couple's poor health or Shelley's most treasured belongings. 'The books in the library are mildewed,' he moaned. The most spacious room became the library, and it was soon filled with his many books. Casts of Apollo and Venus gave it a classical feel.

But Shelley was more enamoured by the area than the house itself. He loved the open air and would, when the weather permitted, spend most of his time outside. He particularly loved the Thames. He had lived on the borders of Windsor Great Park

Percy Bysshe Shelley loved the Thames at Marlow.

for a short spell in 1815 and had gone boating up the river with friend Thomas Love Peacock on one occasion, reaching as far as Lechlade.

It was Peacock, already a resident at Marlow, who persuaded the Shelleys to join him in Buckinghamshire. The two enjoyed numerous rambles together. In *Memoirs of Shelley*, Peacock wrote: 'We took many walks in all directions from Marlow, saw everything worth seeing within a radius of 16 miles.'

The duo would also sometimes walk to London, while, on other occasions, Mary and her father would drive in a gig to some place and meet the walkers. The dreamy poet would often return to the house, his head crowned with wild flowers and Mary would call him 'my elf'.

Though a dreamer and romantic, Shelley had a practical side. He was a young radical and champion of the poor. Schemes of political and social reform were plotted at Albion House and, when Shelley and his many guests finally tired of putting the world to rights, they would turn their attention to literature.

But Shelley was not all talk and no action. He befriended the poor and is even believed to have given away his shoes on one occasion. By the time the Shelleys left Marlow, they too were troubled by debts. Unfortunately, many 'friends' took advantage of the poet's generous disposition.

Marlow was a secluded town when Shelley lived here and he rarely mixed with the locals. He had his own circle of friends and they would generally keep themselves to themselves when they frequented the local inns. Peacock wrote: 'He had no intercourse with his immediate neighbours.' Shelley told his friend: 'I am not wretch enough to tolerate an acquaintance.'

Throughout the summer at Albion House, Shelley worked on *The Revolt of Islam*. The subject matter has no relevance to the beautiful countryside where he penned the work. His pamphlet *Proposal for Putting Reform to the Vote, by the Hermit of Marlow*, also proved he could not lose himself completely in these idyllic surroundings. He wrote several political pamphlets here.

The Revolt of Islam's dedication to Mary points out that those days on the Thames writing the work might not have been so carefree. While it was thought that Shelley was sleeping in his boat, he was at pains to point out that he was working. 'The toil which stole from thee so many an hour . . . Is ended – and the fruit is at thy feet.' He goes on to describe the surroundings: 'Water-falls leap among wild islands green . . . Which framed for my lone boat a lone retreat.'

Throughout the poem there are only snatches of the local scenery, for Shelley believed there were more important things to say. Indeed, the likes of Matthew Arnold and Robert Bridges wrote more about the Thames than he did.

Shelley loved the summer, but the winter in Marlow and that damp house did not appeal. By February 1818, the couple, now in severe financial difficulties, and suffering ill health, sought out a warmer climate.

Percy Bysshe Shelley was never to return to his beloved Thames or even Britain. He drowned in a boating accident in Italy in 1822.

Mary Shelley

Mary Shelley lived in the shadow of her husband during their stay at Marlow, and her neighbours were completely oblivious to what she was plotting behind closed doors. While they watched in wonder at the sometimes-bizarre antics of her husband, the unassuming Mary was at home putting the finishing touches to one of the most popular books in English literature.

The author was still a teenager when she began writing *Frankenstein*. It was published in January 1818, just a month before the Shelleys left Marlow. Mary had already departed their Buckinghamshire home when the first reviews started to appear.

Just 500 copies were printed at the time and the creator of this enduring chiller remained anonymous. Most thought it was the work of her husband, due to the dedication to William Godwin in the book, Mary's father. It received mixed reviews, but its reputation eventually spread and it became what it is today, a classic and perhaps the most famous horror story ever penned.

Mary was not that enamoured with Shelley's plan to move to Marlow and closer to his friend Thomas Love Peacock. She did not hold their new neighbour in very high regard and at first felt uncomfortable in his presence. Peacock had held much affection for Harriet, the poet's first wife who committed suicide, and Mary may have felt she was always competing with her memory.

The Shelleys stayed with Peacock before moving into Albion House, supervising the renovations that were taking place at their new home. Shelley is said to have spent about £1,000 on upholstery, curtains and furniture, despite their growing financial problems. Needless to say, the extravagance was bought on credit. This was Mary's first proper home and the poet wanted to satisfy her taste for elegance.

Albion House, home of the Shelleys.

Mary, like her husband, loved the area and enjoyed visiting the nearby riverside woods, monastic ruins and quiet villages, but she struggled to keep up with Peacock as he rushed the new residents around his favourite spots.

Albion House was always full of visitors, though they were not always welcome. Mary wrote that Peacock came in every day 'uninvited to drink his bottle . . . he morally disgusts me'.

As the financial problems increased, Mary became less happy. She suffered a period of depression after the birth of daughter Clara and, despite the fact that their dream of a happy country existence was coming to an end, she was relieved to be heading off for a new life on the Continent. Sadly, further tragedy was just around the corner, with Percy's death in 1822.

The West Street home of the Shelleys is situated next to Sir William Borlase's Grammar School. It now forms a couple of private residences.

Lord Byron

It appears Marlow has gone too far in its claim that Lord Byron also stayed at Albion House, as the plaque at the Shelleys's former home in West Street suggests to be the case. However, it is generally accepted that Byron never returned to England after leaving its shores in April 1816 and that the Shelleys did not take up residence at Albion House until the following year.

Thomas Love Peacock

Thomas Love Peacock was a man who enjoyed life. His friend Charles Clairmont wrote that he 'was only happy while out from morning till night' and Mary Shelley believed he loved talking, eating and drinking a little too much.

But Peacock still found time to cement his place among the greats of English literature, even if he is little read today. *Nightmare Abbey*, perhaps the author's most famous satirical novel, was written at Marlow, as was the poem *Rhododaphne*. Most of the novelist's characters were modelled on his friends and contemporaries, including Percy Bysshe Shelley.

Most of what we know about Peacock's life during this period is via his connections with the poet. It is thought that he came to the Buckinghamshire town at least a year before his best friend. He was certainly still here when the Shelleys departed and he wrote to them in the spring of 1818, saying that he had no wish to leave Marlow and that Shelley would still find him here on his return from Europe.

Sadly, they never saw each other again and Peacock is thought to have taken up residence in London the following year, before getting married and eventually settling at Lower Halliford, near Shepperton.

Peacock's Marlow house was also in West Street and, like the home of the Shelleys, is now commemorated by a plaque, though the property – No. 47 – has since been converted into a shop. However, the street has at least one more literary connection . . .

T.S. Eliot

The sight of T.S. Eliot on his bike became a common one in Marlow. The poet would cycle to the local railway station in order to catch the train to London, where he worked as a bank clerk in the foreign department at Lloyds.

One of the many plaques in West Street.

Eliot, like the Shelleys and Peacock, also lived in West Street, surely one of the most famous literary streets in the country. His home – No. 31 – is now a restaurant, but there is also a plaque high on the wall above the shop front.

Bertrand Russell had a financial stake in the cottage and arranged for the Eliots to come here towards the end of the First World War. The poet would spend his weekends in the garden reading and writing. His wife Vivien was particularly attached to their home. Aldous Huxley was among the literary visitors.

G.P.R. James

The 'Little Devil' – the name given to G.P.R. James by his friend Lord Byron because of his headstrong personality and love of adventure – lived at Quoitings in Oxford Road during the 1830s.

James was a prolific writer of romantic historical novels. He was one of the best-known writers of the first half of the nineteenth century and had a wide circle of literary friends, but is all but forgotten today.

Frank E. Smedley

Nineteenth-century novelist Francis Edward Smedley, who often appeared in print as Frank E. Smedley, was another native of Marlow. He was born in High Street and, just before his death, bought Beechwood, a country house on the outskirts of the town.

Smedley, a cripple from childhood, penned high-spirited novels of sport and adventure, including *Frank Fairlegh*, which is best remembered for the enduring phrase: 'All's fair in love and war.'

Jerome K. Jerome

Jerome K. Jerome knew the Thames – and Marlow in particular – very well. He described Marlow as 'one of the pleasantest river centres I know of' in his most famous work, *Three Men in a Boat*. He added: 'It is a bustling, lively little town; not very picturesque on the whole, it is true, but there are many quiet nooks and corners to be found in it.' It was at Marlow where Montmorency the dog makes 'an awful ass of himself' following a confrontation with a cat.

Jerome lived at a number of properties in Marlow over the years, the most notable being Monks Corner at Marlow Common. He lived here from 1910–20. Nearby Wood End House was another former residence.

Many pubs also claim the author wrote *Three Men in a Boat* within their walls, including The Two Brewers in St Peter Street. The novel was a huge success when it was published in 1889 and remains enormously popular today.

William Morris

William Morris was another writer to take his characters on a trip along the Thames. In *News from Nowhere*, his Utopian romance, the narrator wakes in the future, a Communist paradise. The work includes a poetic evocation of a journey up the Thames from London through a countryside untouched by industrialisation.

The travellers get out of their boat at Marlow, or Bisham on the other side of the river, to be exact. The journey concludes at Kelmscott Manor, near Lechlade, Morris's country home from 1871.

The Two Brewers, where a classic was supposedly penned.

The Compleat Angler hotel on the banks of the Thames at Marlow is named after the most famous work of Izaak Walton. Walton first published his musings on fishing in 1653 and it has become one of the most reprinted books in English literature.

The present hotel is believed to have started life as a small inn in the early seventeenth century. Edgar Wallace, Noel Coward and J.M. Barrie were among its more recent guests.

American theatre manager and playwright Charles Frohman loved Marlow and rented a cottage here each summer. He was a close friend of J.M. Barrie and produced *Peter Pan*. A memorial statue in The Causeway honours Frohman, who died in the sinking of the *Lusitania* in 1915.

MEDMENHAM

Hell-Fire Club

Medmenham Abbey was reputed to be the first headquarters of the notorious eighteenth-century Hell-Fire Club. Though there is evidence to suggest this group of eminent men met earlier in London, there is no doubting the abbey, which no longer exists, was their main meeting place before West Wycombe Caves.

Francis Dashwood, owner of West Wycombe House, founded the Brotherhood of St Francis of Wycombe. The organisation had many names. The group became known as The Order of the Knights of St Francis, or simply the Monks of Medmenham, though now most refer to it as the Hell-Fire Club, despite the fact that members never used that title themselves.

The Compleat Angler is named in honour of Izaak Walton.

Dressed in the habits of monks, the men would partake in salubrious activities. Tales of wild orgies and black magic were fed to tourists many years after the demise of the organisation and the deaths of its members. A number of literary figures were associated with the club, while other writers, including Charles Dickens, wrote about it.

The few ruined walls that remain of the abbey now form part of a private residence at the bottom of Ferry Lane.

Basil Liddell Hart

Basil Liddell Hart, one of Britain's leading military historians, was buried at Medmenham, following his death in 1970. He was the author of the official manual on drill and tactics, as well as a number of other works. His grave can be found in the churchyard at St Peter & St Paul's Church.

HAMBLEDEN

Francis Quarles

Religious poet Francis Quarles wrote the words inscribed on the tomb of Sister Martha, who lies at rest in the parish church at pretty Hambleden. Quarles became the wife of Cope D'Oyley, a prominent landowner. Her brother is best remembered for *Emblems*, a very successful collection of devotional poems, and the most popular of the seventeenth-century emblem books, works consisting of symbolic illustrations.

Basil Liddell Hart is buried at Medmenham.

GREENLANDS

William Henry Smith

It is not with a pen that William Henry Smith made such an impact on the literary world – but he made a lot of money out of a lot of writers. Shorten his name to W.H. Smith and there will be few who have not heard of his legacy.

Smith lived in an imposing riverside house. Jerome K. Jerome, in *Three Men in a Boat*, mentioned both Smith and his property. The author described Greenlands, near Hambleden, as 'the rather uninteresting-looking river residence of my newsagent – a quiet unassuming old gentleman'.

However, the influence Smith had on the literary world cannot be overstated. He secured exclusive rights to erect bookstalls at all the important railway stations in England. Smith, the son of strict Methodists, took a very moral stand on the types of books stocked. He insisted that all pernicious literature, for which these bookstalls had been notorious, was to be excluded, a stance which continued after Smith's death. The company, which was actually set up by Smith's father, refused to stock the controversial *Jude the Obscure* and helped end Thomas Hardy's novel-writing career in the process. Hardy, angered by the snub and harsh words from the critics, never wrote another novel.

Greenlands is now a college. The present building was built in the nineteenth century, but a house has stood here for many centuries.

Bulstrode Whitelocke

Greenlands was once in the hands of lawyer and diplomat Bulstrode Whitelocke, one of the most influential men of the seventeenth century. Whitelocke, who owned various properties in the area, notably Fawley Court further along the river at Henley-on-Thames, was a prominent Parliamentarian, serving Oliver Cromwell during the Civil War. Though not remembered for his literary efforts, his annals in particular serve as a useful insight into the troubled politics of the era. He was also the author of other political and theological works.

8

Just Over the Border

Buckinghamshire is bordered by six counties. Mention must be made of some of the many literary associations 'just over the border', particularly those within the Chilterns, an area blessed by an abundance of scribes over the years.

Buckinghamshire is the county most associated with the Chilterns, but the region also takes in part of Bedfordshire and Hertfordshire to the north, and stretches as far as Berkshire and Oxfordshire to the south.

The far western tip of Hertfordshire pierces Buckinghamshire. The town of Berkhamsted, in particular, can claim more than its fair share of writers for its own, including one of the most popular novelists of the twentieth century.

On the south side of the Thames, in Berkshire, some of the country's best-loved children's characters were created, while further along the famous river into Oxfordshire, and inland to Thame – site of some spooky goings-on – there are further literary delights, all within a mile or so of the Buckinghamshire boundary.

BERKHAMSTED

William Cowper

Prominent men in history have graced Berkhamsted, kings and princes once residing within the now-ruined walls of its castle. However, scribe Robert Southey once declared: 'This little town will be more known in after ages as the birthplace of William Cowper than for its connection with so many historical personages who figured in the tragedies of old.'

There is no doubting the affection that poet and hymn-writer William Cowper held for Berkhamsted. Though particularly fond of Buckinghamshire, where he spent much of his adult life, he also enjoyed some of his happiest days here and it broke his heart when his ties with the town were finally severed following the death of his father. He wrote: 'Then, and not till then, I felt for the first time that I and my native place were disunited for ever.'

Cowper was in his late teens when his father died. He was called from London, but arrived home just after the Revd John Cowper passed away. The poet spent a few months at the rectory, his early childhood home, but then left for good. He said he 'sighed a long adieu to fields and woods from which I once thought I should never be parted' before taking his leave.

Cowper's many letters and poems highlight his love of the area. He wrote: 'There was neither tree, nor gate, nor stile in all that country, to which I did not feel a relation, and the house itself I preferred to a palace.' In *On the Receipt of My Mother's Picture out of Norfolk*, he describes 'Gardener Robin' walking him to school, a small, private establishment that once stood on the site of 212 High Street. The rector's gardener would lead him each day, hand in hand, the youngster 'wrapt in scarlet mantle warm, and velvet capt'.

Berkhamsted still has many reminders of perhaps its greatest son. The Church of St Peter, where his father preached, contains a memorial window to the poet. The church also has a memorial to his mother and other members of the family. A number of roads are also named in honour of the author.

The house Cowper preferred to a palace, which was situated in Rectory Lane, has long gone. Sadly, the Revd John Crofts, who was the rector of St Peter's for some forty years in the first half of the nineteenth century, pulled it down and built a new rectory.

The Berkhamsted church William Cowper knew so well.

Graham Greene

Novelist Graham Greene was writing about his own childhood when he declared that we are all 'emigrants from a country we remember too little of'. It is perhaps ironic he should think this way. Indeed, for someone who had difficulty recalling his schooldays in Berkhamsted, Greene still penned an awful lot on the experience. His novels, poems, non-fiction and letters are full of references from that 'country of childhood'.

In truth, it is hardly surprising Greene should turn to his years at Berkhamsted for inspiration in latter life. School to him was more than just a place you went to each day – it was also his home. Greene was born at the school he later attended, and lived there too.

Charles Greene, father of Graham, was second master at Berkhamsted School when his son was born in the family home attached to it in 1904. That home was St John's House, a boarders' house, which is situated in Chesham Road, a short walk from the main school building.

When Charles was made headmaster, the family left St John's for School House, a home attached to the main building in Castle Street. School House was the family home until Greene Senior retired in 1927. Unfortunately for young Graham, it ceased to be his home much earlier. The author was almost 14 when he became a boarder at St John's, the place of his birth. There was no privacy or comforts in a dormitory and Greene, not helped by the fact his father was headmaster, was a victim of bullies.

Greene recalled his time here again and again in his work. *England Made Me*, *Brighton Rock*, *The Lawless Roads*, *The Confidential Agent*, *The Ministry of Fear*, *The Lost Childhood* and, of course, his successful autobiography *A Sort of Life* are just some of the works that draw on his school experiences. In *The Lawless Roads*, Greene quotes a line from a sermon on hell to describe his schooldays. He also planned to write a novel about a school, but abandoned the idea because 'I couldn't bear mentally living again several years in these surroundings'. Instead, Greene gained his 'revenge' on many of his bullies by immortalising them as characters in his books, many of whom are not dealt a good hand in life.

The author's writing career was just beginning to bloom at Berkhamsted. *The Berkhamstedian*, the school's own magazine, published several of his early stories and he was even showing off some new-found London literary friends. Poet Walter de la Mare came to the school for tea with Greene and his parents, and the young Graham proudly posed as the poet's friend.

Greene left Berkhamsted in 1922 to further his education at Oxford, and it was here his literary career really took off. Berkhamsted can certainly claim a part in shaping his writing, however. Its streets and buildings, as well as historical incidents, are recalled in numerous works. In the short story, *The Innocent*, the narrator goes back to his home town, Bishop's Hendron, which is clearly Berkhamsted, while the town becomes Denton in the unfinished novel, *Across the Border*.

There is no doubt Berkhamsted had a hold on Greene. He later said: 'Everything one was to become must have been there, for better or worse.'

One of Graham Greene's contemporaries at Berkhamsted School was poet, critic and historian Peter Quennell. He became the editor of the *Cornhill Magazine* and wrote biographies on a number of writers.

Berkhamsted School was home to Graham Greene, and also his birthplace.

J.M. Barrie

Respectable Berkhamsted, at the heart of commuter country, is not exactly Never Land. But the Llewelyn Davies family – the inspiration for the chief characters in J.M. Barrie's *Peter Pan* – came here in search of a new life. They left their home in the capital while Barrie was busy working on the stage show, which opened in 1904.

Barrie had less time to visit his dear friends, but he did come to Berkhamsted as often as he could and was well known in the town. The family lived at Egerton House, an Elizabethan mansion in High Street, which no longer exists, the Rex Cinema now standing in its place.

Mr and Mrs Llewelyn Davies were the inspiration for Mr and Mrs Darling, while their boys, even though one was actually named Peter, all helped inspire the title character, according to the playwright. The spark for Peter was achieved 'by rubbing the five of you violently together, as savages with two sticks produce flame', Barrie later told the children. When one of them was too ill to get to the capital to see the show one year, the author brought the production to Egerton House, complete with London set and cast.

Following the death of Mr Llewelyn Davies in 1907, Barrie continued to support the family, eventually bringing them back to London. Mrs Llewelyn Davies was the daughter of George du Maurier, author of *Trilby*.

Geoffrey Chaucer

It is not really known whether Geoffrey Chaucer ever visited Berkhamsted Castle. There is, however, a good chance that he did. Chaucer was appointed clerk of the works to Richard II for a period and it is quite likely that he had cause to visit the royal residence on occasions.

Little remains of the castle today, other than its massive earthworks and a few ruined walls.

Other former Berkhamsted residents include hymn-writer Henry Twells, historian G.M. Trevelyan, short-story writer W.W. Jacobs and children's author H.E. Todd, who gained fame for the Bobby Brewster books.

NORTHCHURCH

Maria Edgeworth

It is not really a surprise that novelist Maria Edgeworth should later title one of her works *The Parent's Assistant*. No doubt she would have been exactly that when she came home to Northchurch during school holidays.

Her father, Richard Lovell Edgeworth, himself a writer, is believed to have married four times and produced at least nineteen children, so there were always little ones around while Maria was growing up. She was still very young when her own mother died. Her father is said to have brought her stepmother and the rest of the family to Northchurch in 1776, when Maria was about 9.

Though the family only stayed for a few years, The Limes – now named Edgeworth House in honour of its famous former occupants – held many fond memories for Maria, who became one of the most popular novelists of her time.

Castle Rackrent, which brought the author instant fame, has a strong Hertfordshire interest, the story of Lady Cathcart of Tewin one of the inspirations for the novel. Edgeworth House is situated on the main road between Northchurch and Berkhamsted.

Maria also certainly knew all about the area's most famous inhabitant and was one of many to later write about Peter the Wild Boy, as he was known. Peter was discovered in a field in Germany. He could only grunt like an animal and fed on fruit, roots and buds. George I brought him to England and the country became captivated by the strange creature that walked barefoot and rested, animal-fashion, on his knees and elbows. When the royal court became bored of their new 'pet', he was entrusted to the care of a maid who arranged for him to live with a farmer in the Berkhamsted area.

The newspapers ensured Peter became a celebrity and curious visitors continued to flock to the region to meet him. It is believed he led an inoffensive life, but was prone to wandering. His new 'owners' fitted him with a collar with instructions that a reward would be offered should anyone find and return him.

Peter died in his 70s and was buried at St Mary's Church, Northchurch. His simple tombstone is close to the church porch.

Maria Edgeworth was not the only author to write about Peter the Wild Boy. Daniel Defoe wrote an account of his early life and many say he inspired Jonathan Swift to create the Yahoos in *Gulliver's Travels*. Swift was certainly fascinated by him and wrote much on the subject. Charles Dickens also mentions Peter in *Martin Chuzzlewit* and *The Mystery of Edwin Drood*. Thomas Day, a frequent visitor to the Edgeworth home in Northchurch, was probably thinking about him when penning *The History of Little Jack*, a moral tale about a boy suckled by goats.

Peter the Wild Boy inspired many writers.

Thomas Bland, headmaster of Berkhamsted School in the latter half of the eighteenth century, was incensed by the way gossipers and jokers treated Peter. He blamed writers for being a little too liberal with the truth. 'Men of some eminence in the literary world have in their works published strange opinions and ill-founded conjectures,' he said. Bland published his own 'true account' of Peter's life.

LITTLE GADDESDEN

Geoffrey Chaucer

The work of doctor, priest and writer John of Gaddesden could not fail to attract attention. Geoffrey Chaucer mentioned this eccentric in the prologue to *The Canterbury Tales*.

Chaucer may have visited Berkhamsted Castle as clerk of the works to Richard II, so he would have got to know the local area, and stories about this incredible man would, at very least, have been passed on through the royal court.

John of Gaddesden was an eminent fourteenth-century medical writer. He served Edward I and was also court physician to Edward II. His literary fame rests on his book of charms and cures. *Rosa Medicinae*, or *Rosa Anglica* as it later became known, lists diseases and remedies, while also giving practical advice on health and cooking. Most of the cures involve ingredients usually found in a witch's cauldron. The author believed medicine should remain a mystery and that the uneducated should not ask questions, which is probably just as well, considering what they were told to do in order to get well. Cures might involve hanging the heart of a bird around one's neck or applying animal droppings to a wound!

Chaucer probably visited Berkhamsted Castle.

The doctor in *The Canterbury Tales* is particularly fond of his fees and John is believed to have also been that way inclined. He is said to have received a very large payment from the barber-surgeons for a prescription in which the chief ingredients were frogs.

There is a property on the corner of Church Road opposite the entrance to Ashridge Park known as John O'Gaddesden's House. It is believed to stand on the site of the original home of this colourful character.

ASHRIDGE

John Skelton

'A pleasanter place than Ashridge is, hard were to find.' So wrote court poet John Skelton after one visit in the early 1520s. It is not really known whether his stay here was a passing visit, but he certainly enjoyed it enough to pen those words in *The Garland of Laurel*. Skelton was a huge admirer of Geoffrey Chaucer, so may have come to the area to retrace his steps.

The Ashridge estate consists of some 5,000 acres of woodland and commons. It is one of the most beautiful parts of the Chilterns.

John Milton

John Milton had yet to make a name for himself when he wrote a masque for patron John Egerton, the 1st Earl of Bridgewater and owner of Ashridge House. The poet penned *Comus* to celebrate the institution of Egerton as president of

John O'Gaddesden's House.

John Skelton liked what he saw at Ashridge.

the Council of Wales. The official ceremony took place at Ludlow Castle in 1634 and the spectacular evening of entertainment – attended by gentry and nobility – concluded with Milton's masque.

Ashridge House, now a college, has received many literary guests over the years, notably at the end of the nineteenth and beginning of the twentieth centuries. Lady Adelaide Brownlow had a wide range of friends and welcomed a never-ending stream of 'celebrities', including writers and members of royalty. Among the scribes to have visited were John Ruskin, Oscar Wilde, H.G. Wells and E.F. Benson.

ALDBURY

Mrs Humphry Ward

Charming Aldbury is not the sort of place you would expect to inspire a novelist. It appears to be a typical English country village where not very much happens. But Mary Augusta Ward – better known as Mrs Humphry Ward – found plenty to fuel the juices of her imagination when she moved here. She based many of her characters on real people, and some of her plots were inspired by true-life incidents that had occurred in the locality, and no incident was too disturbing to immortalise in print. Her novel *Marcella* draws upon the brutal murders of two gamekeepers that took place close to her home the year before she moved into the village.

Aldbury itself is perhaps best immortalised in *The Story of Bessie Costrell*, when it appears in the guise of Clinton Magna. The author is said to have penned the work in just over two weeks and she herself called it a 'grimy little tragedy'. The story of a woman who drowned herself in the public well at Aldbury is thought to have been Mrs Ward's inspiration on this occasion.

The Chilterns clearly inspired the author and the many works she penned while living here. Even her final novel, *Harvest*, draws on her wartime experiences at Stocks, her Aldbury home. She certainly did her bit for the war effort. Not only did she share vegetables from Stocks with the villagers, but she also put out a cow to graze on the local cricket pitch in order to provide fresh milk for her neighbours.

Mrs Ward is little read today, but she was one of the most popular novelists of her time. She came from a literary background and was surrounded by writers throughout her life. She was the niece of Matthew Arnold; mother-in-law of historian G.M. Trevelyan and aunt to Aldous Huxley and Julian Huxley, who both spent many happy school holidays visiting her at Stocks. Aldous later admitted that Mrs Ward had been a kind of literary godmother to him. Other guests included Henry James and George Bernard Shaw, who lived at Ayot St Lawrence, a few miles north of St Albans.

Mrs Ward had already enjoyed literary success (*Robert Elsmere* was published in 1888 and remains her most popular novel) when she moved to Stocks with her husband. The house was chosen for its seclusion and was blessed with a huge walled garden in which she would write. The author loved the property at first sight and said herself that those early days at Aldbury were among the happiest of her life, though she suffered much ill health here. She lived at Stocks from 1892 until her death in 1920, and was laid to rest at the parish church, where her grave can be seen.

Stocks House is now the headquarters of a golf and country club.

Mrs Ward drew on charming Aldbury's darker side.

Mrs Ward is buried in the parish churchyard.

Louis MacNeice

The twentieth-century poet Louis MacNeice lived in Aldbury for a spell towards the end of his life. He and actress Mary Wimbush set up home at 39 Stocks Road, after buying three cottages and knocking them into one. MacNeice frequented the Greyhound Inn, where his favourite spot was under the clock in the public bar. It is believed *The Burning Perch*, which appeared in 1963, was penned in Aldbury.

Walter Scott may have been another visitor to Stocks. His good friend James Adam Gordon was a former owner of the house in the first half of the nineteenth century. It is possible that Scott heard of the village of Ivinghoe, which he used for the title *Ivanhoe*, while here.

TRING

George Eliot

George Eliot immortalised a fellow literary figure and friend in one of her most famous novels. Among the hundreds employed at the silk mill in Tring, which

141

Poet Louis MacNeice's Aldbury home.

first opened in 1824, was Chartist poet Gerald Massey, the son of a poor canal boatman. It is believed he became the inspiration for the title character in *Felix Holt the Radical*.

Massey the Poet, as he was known, was born in a wharf on the canal close to Tring in 1828 and educated at a charity school in the town. He was put to work at the silk mill when he was just 8 years old, and endured long days in grim conditions. His tough upbringing was reflected in his poetry, which expressed his strong socialist views. He was wholly committed to the cause of the peasant labourer.

Massey, who later moved to a cottage in the nearby village of Little Gaddesden, eventually settled in London and is buried in the capital.

The mill at Tring ultimately closed, but Lord Rothschild, a name much associated with the area, ran it at a loss for some time when the silk trade fell into decline in order to prevent his employees from becoming destitute. It was eventually converted into a generating station and is now in multiple use. The old building can still be seen from Brook Street.

William Cobbett

Essayist and political reformer William Cobbett was a visitor to Tring and had only good words for it. He wrote: 'Everything at this pretty town pleased me exceedingly.' The writer dined at the Rose & Crown in 1829 and was so impressed with the whole affair, addressed everyone for ninety minutes.

Cobbett gained fame in the literary world for *Rural Rides*, an account of his many travels.

William Cobbett dined at the Rose & Crown.

CHORLEYWOOD

Oscar Wilde

Respectable Chorleywood has a connection with one of the most scandalous figures in literature – Oscar Wilde. Actor-manager George Alexander had a part to play in Wilde's rise to fame, but has also been criticised for deserting him during his darkest days.

Alexander, who lived and died at Chorleywood, ran the famous St James's Theatre in London. He persuaded Wilde to pen some of his most famous plays. However, his loyalty and sincerity came under question after the playwright was convicted for homosexuality. Alexander is said to have continued to profit from the author with little regard for him. He tried to keep the production of *The Importance of Being Earnest* from closing by removing the shamed writer's name from the programme and posters. Staff at the theatre, including Alexander, are also said to have refused to give evidence on behalf of Wilde. These incidents caused a rift between the two that is believed to have lasted a number of years.

Of course, Alexander was not the only one to turn their back on Wilde and it appears he made amends. He later provided the author with voluntary payments for the plays he had acquired cheaply during the latter's bankruptcy, which were being staged again, and also bequeathed the rights to Wilde's sons. And, during happier times, Wilde did not do too badly out of Alexander. The latter frequently gave the writer money in advance for work that the playwright often took ages to complete. He famously offered Wilde £1,000 for the rights to *Lady Windermere's Fan*, the first major play he produced at St James's Theatre

George Alexander knew all about the importance of being earnest.

in 1892. Wilde replied: 'I have such excellent confidence in your judgement, my dear Alec, I have no alternative but to refuse.' The canny author wanted a percentage and he got it. Such was the success of the play, it proved to be a shrewd move.

Alexander, unlike Wilde, is little remembered today. Most Chorleywood residents are oblivious to the fact this once influential man, who can claim a part in the rise of one of the most famous figures in literature, lies at rest in their village.

Alexander lived at Tollgate Cottage for a spell before moving into Little Court, a grander property further along Rickmansworth Road, which he himself built in 1911. It is now known as The Court and sits virtually next to Christ Church, where Alexander and his wife are buried. Staff at St James's Theatre carried the coffin following his death in 1918.

Quaker scribe William Penn, the founder of Pennsylvania, married his first wife, Gulielma Springett, at King John's Farm in Shepherds Lane, a well-preserved timbered house. They settled at nearby Rickmansworth.

COOKHAM DEAN

Kenneth Grahame

'The wafts from his old home pleaded, whispered, conjured, and finally claimed him imperiously.' Kenneth Grahame was describing Mole in this extract from *The Wind in the Willows*, but it could have been himself. Just like his famous creation, the author also could not resist returning 'home'. Happy childhood days at Cookham Dean left such a lasting impression on Grahame, he returned to live in the village as an adult. 'Coming back here wakens every recollection,' he said. He went on: 'I feel I should never be surprised to meet myself as I was when a little chap of five, suddenly coming round the corner.'

It is easy to imagine the young boy 'messing about in boats' at Cookham Dean, a pleasant village on the south side of the Thames, which perhaps has the strongest claim to being the 'birthplace' of *The Wind in the Willows*.

The couple of years or so the young Grahame spent at The Mount, a spacious property with large grounds, were among his happiest. He came to the home of his maternal grandmother, 'Granny Ingles', in 1864 following the death of his mother. He used to go down to the river with his uncle, the Revd David Ingles, a fine rower who played a huge part in instilling Grahame's love of nature and the Thames. Sadly, the family left Cookham Dean in the spring of 1866 for a smaller home at Winkfield, near Cranbourne, but the village remained forever etched in the memory.

Grahame enjoyed a career in the Bank of England before making his name with his pen. The author painted an unsentimental picture of childhood in *The Golden Age* and *Dream Days*, two books published towards the end of the nineteenth century. In these works, adults were often out of touch with the real concerns of children. That is a label most would not attach to Grahame, however. He knew exactly what children wanted to read, if his classic novel is anything to go by.

The Wind in the Willows was published in 1908. The Grahame family had moved to Cookham Dean at this stage. They were to reside at Mayfield between 1906 and 1910.

Look out for Mole, Rat and Toad.

The book began life as simple bedtime stories for the author's own son and later continued in a series of letters. It is incredible to think that Mole, Rat and Toad, who are now known to both children and adults throughout the world, were originally created for just one person.

Grahame never drew straight from life and the exact locations for the adventures of these perennial favourites could have, arguably, been gleaned from any river and not necessarily the Thames. Even Cornwall, the destination for many family holidays, claims to be an inspiration for the book. Nevertheless, the Thames must surely have been the biggest influence. The Wild Wood, home of the stoats, could easily be Quarry Wood, a little upstream from Cookham Dean, while Toad Hall may be a mixture of any of the grand properties in the area, including Mapledurham, Cliveden and Harleyford Manor, even though Mapledurham is generally accepted to have the strongest claim.

There is a plaque in memory of the author at Herries School in Dean Lane. Mayfield was incorporated into part of the school building. Grahame spent the final years of his life further along the Thames at Pangbourne. The River & Rowing Museum at Henley-on-Thames features a permanent walk-through attraction devoted to Grahame's classic tale.

HENLEY-ON-THAMES

George Orwell

The first real British home of Eric Blair, better known as George Orwell, was in bustling Henley-on-Thames. The writer moved to Oxfordshire from India while still very young.

The family first lived at Ermadale in Vicarage Road, a spacious house less than a mile from the river. A move to The Nutshell, close by in Western Road, followed, before the Blairs left for Shiplake just a couple of miles away, which became the young Eric's favourite Oxfordshire residence. Even when the family returned to Henley after some three years, moving to a smaller property in St Mark's Road, Eric would regularly cycle to and from Shiplake in order to play with the close friends he had made there.

Charles Dickens

The Thames features much in the work of Charles Dickens. Though the London and eastern stretches of the river receive the most attention, the upper reaches in Oxfordshire are not overlooked.

The river dominates *Our Mutual Friend*. It is thought The Paper Mill, where Lizzie Hexam works, is based on Marsh Mill at Henley-on-Thames. It is also on the towpath here that Bradley Headstone attempts to murder Eugene Wrayburn.

Jerome K. Jerome wrote that Henley 'was full of bustle' and getting ready for its famous Regatta when the heroes of *Three Men in a Boat* arrived here. They have trouble finding their vessel after an evening out in the town.

Jerome K. Jerome knew all about Henley and its Regatta.

STONOR

Edmund Campion

Stonor, the magnificent estate just north of Henley-on-Thames, became the base for one of the most famous literary counter-attacks against Protestantism. The Catholic family of Stonor have been associated with the house for centuries and it became the hiding place for persecuted priests in times of trouble.

The most famous to take refuge within its walls was the Jesuit martyr Edmund Campion. He came in 1581 as the guest of Dame Cecily Stonor and here used a secret printing press to launch perhaps the best-known counter-attack against the Protestant reformers. His pamphlet – *Decem Rationes (Ten Reasons)* – outlined his controversial views on the invalidity of the Established Church following the Reformation. Campion himself distributed copies in Oxford and, such was the outrage it caused, a major search for the instigator was soon launched.

The author was eventually captured near Wantage. Under torture, the role of the Stonor family was revealed. The printing press was removed and many involved in the scheme, including Dame Cecily, were either imprisoned or exiled. Campion suffered an even crueller fate. He was hanged, drawn and quartered later that year, though the Catholic Church made him a saint in the twentieth century.

The house and gardens at Stonor are open to the public.

Robert Parsons – who went on to write *The Christian Directory* – is thought to have been one of those involved in the secret printing operation at Stonor. It is believed he had left by the time the estate was raided and later escaped to the Continent, where he published his most famous work.

Stonor hides a literary secret.

CROWELL

Thomas Ellwood

Quaker poet Thomas Ellwood, the loyal friend of John Milton, was born in the tiny village of Crowell in 1639. In *The History of the Life of Thomas Ellwood – Written by Himself*, the author tells us that he came into the world during troubled times. His father was a Parliamentarian and, fearing for their safety, moved the family to London, which was held by that particular party at the time. Thomas was 'carried' off to the capital at about the age of two and did not return home until his father considered it safe to do so. On his return, he attended Thame Grammar School, but Mr Ellwood Senior curtailed his education in order to ensure that there were sufficient funds for Thomas's elder brother to finish his studies at Oxford. From here, it appears the unfortunate youngster went to wait on Lord Wenman at Thame Park.

The writer was to experience much persecution following his conversion to Quakerism, including beatings from his own father who could not understand why his son would not remove his hat in his presence.

Ellwood House stands on the busy B4009, which runs through Crowell.

THAME

W.B. Yeats

Visitors to Thame are unlikely to find too many things out of the ordinary here. It is a pleasant town and not universally known for strange goings-on.

However, W.B. Yeats might have disagreed when he lived here for a few months in the summer of 1921. The poet, who was known for his love of the mystical, was apparently surrounded by phenomena. He reported various bizarre happenings and he was not the only one. Even the servants complained about the whistling sounds, which Yeats believed were made by his spiritual advisers. Others claimed they could also smell the scent of flowers, even though none were actually in the house. There were reputedly also flashes of light and the occasional striking of a chair, while, on the corner of the street, a warm breath seemed to come up from the ground.

Yeats came to Cuttlebrook House with his wife George and daughter Anne in July. The family had spent the previous few months at nearby Shillingford, after renting out their home in Oxford. Their new abode – situated in High Street opposite the old grammar school – was owned by three spinsters and their mother.

It was certainly an atmospheric house, full of various clutter accumulated over many generations. Yeats commented on the guns and swords on the top floor. He said the house reminded him of his childhood in Sligo. The family welcomed a new arrival in August. Their son Michael, it was said, was born to the unseasonable smell of roses.

Following a visit to Dublin in September, the family returned to their home in Oxford before finally moving to Ireland.

Poet W.B. Yeats lived at Cuttlebrook House.

The Spread Eagle entertained many writers.

John Fothergill

The eccentric John Fothergill surprised all that knew him when he abandoned his life as a scholar to run an inn. In 1922, he became 'Pioneer Amateur Innkeeper' of the Spread Eagle, which is situated in Thame's town centre. He ran the establishment for some ten years and recorded his experiences in *An Innkeeper's Diary*, which was published in 1931.

Many writers frequented the Spread Eagle, such as G.K. Chesterton, George Bernard Shaw, H.G. Wells, Rebecca West and Evelyn Waugh. Dora Carrington, a writer as well as an artist, is said to have painted the inn sign for Fothergill.

J.R.R. Tolkien

If you go down to the woods today you may be in for a big surprise. You could certainly bump into a giant or a dragon during your stroll in Ham Wood on the outskirts of Thame. Farmer Giles did. This is where J.R.R. Tolkien set the adventures of his reluctant red-bearded hero who gains great wealth by out-witting both a giant and a dragon.

Even though *Farmer Giles of Ham* is a fable, it is set in the Thames Valley and is thought to be the only time the author based one of his books on a known region. Ham Wood is situated just north of Thame. A number of other places in the area are also mentioned in the work, including the town itself. Tolkien lived most of his life at nearby Oxford and would no doubt have known the area very well.

Farmer Giles of Ham is no *The Lord of the Rings*, but this charming and light-hearted short story, which was published in 1949, is clearly the work of the same author. It bears numerous similarities to *The Hobbit*, in particular, with

Thame Grammar School bred many literary greats.

Farmer Giles displaying many characteristics of Bilbo Baggins, the hero of that particular tale.

Thame Grammar School can claim many men of letters among its former pupils, particularly in the seventeenth century. Ex-students include poet William Basse, poet and bishop Henry King, dramatist Shackerley Marmion, author and divine Dr John Fell, antiquary Anthony à Wood, Quaker poet Thomas Ellwood and dramatist George Etherege.

John Hampden, who has been the subject of many writers, was also taught at the school. The house where he died after being wounded at the Battle of Chalgrove Field is situated along Thame's main street, opposite the town hall, where there is a memorial.

This is where our particular journey ends, but we could have travelled a few extra miles to explore John Bunyan Country in Bedfordshire, or further north into Northamptonshire, a county associated with the poet John Dryden. Even Middlesex, the most urban of Buckinghamshire's neighbours, can lay claim to once being home to some of our best-loved authors, such as George Orwell, who taught at Uxbridge.

To the very south is Windsor and Eton, two towns that could fill a book in their own right. Eton College, in particular, can claim a part in producing some of the country's greatest literary talent. And, of course, the Buckinghamshire border is only six miles or so from an even greater seat of learning – the University of Oxford.

However, these stories must be left for someone else to tell.

Index